Worship
When God Walks Among Us

OTHER BOOKS BY
DR. SHERLOCK BALLY:

DEALING WITH THE
STORMS OF LIFE

ENDUED AND MANTLED

FROM TRIALS TO TRIUMPH

PSALM 102 AND
THE LAST DAYS PROPHECIES

GLORY
WHERE ATMOSPHERES COLLIDE

*This book
along with all of the above titles
are available at amazon.com
and other retailers.*

Worship
When God Walks Among Us

By
Dr. Sherlock Bally

Logos to Rhema Publishing
11063-D South Memorial Drive # 346
Tulsa, OK 74133

Copyright
Worship When God Walks Among Us©2013 Dr. Sherlock Bally
All Rights Reserved

No part of this publication (book) may be reproduced, stored in a retrieval system, or be transmitted in any form, or by any means, electronic, mechanical, photocopying or otherwise without the prior written consent of the author, Dr. Sherlock Bally, or the publisher, Logos To Rhema Publishing.

Written permission must be secured from the publisher or the author to use or reproduce any part of this book, except for the inclusion of brief quotations in critical reviews or articles.

Unless otherwise noted, all Scripture taken from

THE KING JAMES VERSION

ISBN -10:
ISBN -13:

Published in the
United States of America by

Susan K. Reidel
Logos to Rhema Publishing
11063-D South Memorial Drive # 346
Tulsa, OK 74133
(918) 606-5346

Contents

	Preface	7
Chapter 1	Worship as an Ascent	9
Chapter 2	Heaven Reached: Earth Touched	29
Chapter 3	The Crucified I	41
Chapter 4	When God Walks Among Us	57
Chapter 5	The Ark of the Covenant: The Heart of God	85
Chapter 6	The Sacrifice and the Sequence	109
Chapter 7	The Ark-The Cherubim God's Meeting Place	131
Chapter 8	Take Him Up To Let Him Down	141
Chapter 9	When God Walks in Your Furnace	153

Preface

One of the predominant truths that are woven into the fabric of scripture from Genesis to Revelation is the thought that God desires to walk among us. The purpose of the offerings of the Old Testament, the entrance into the tabernacle, to the Holy of Holies fully illustrates the heart of God to come and abide with His people. From the walking in the garden of Eden to His dwelling with His people in the New Jerusalem, the thought of being among the people is prominent. This book will give a perspective of worship that is a vital connection to this powerful truth of God walking amongst us. Worship has carried the idea of an ascent to God. In this book, we will go a step further and show that the ascent to God through worship is preparatory for a descent of God to the worshipper. Be blessed as you read the revelation of Worship, When God Walks Among Us.

Chapter 1

Worship as an Ascent

The thought that worship leads me into an ascent is a revolutionary principle. The world with all its tentacles and traps that are founded on the lust of the flesh, the lust of the eyes and the pride of life, is impotent to restrict the worshipper. In one millisecond, as my gaze is refocused from earth to heaven, and my spirit begins to extol the Lord of Lords, this world is no longer my prison.

I John 2:14-18 states, *"I have written unto you, fathers, because ye have known him that is from the beginning. I have written unto you, young men, because ye are strong, and the word of God abideth in you, and ye have overcome the wicked one. Love not the world, neither the things that are in the world. If any man love the world, the love of the Father is not in him. For all that is in the world, the lust of the flesh, and the lust of the eyes, and the pride of life, is not of the Father, but is of the world. And the world passeth away, and the lust thereof: but he that doeth the will of God abideth forever. Little children, it is the last time: and as ye have heard that antichrist shall come, even now are there many antichrists; whereby we know that it is the last time."*

The Bible exposes the world behind the world, the force behind the force, and the system behind the system. All we see is the physical material world of machinery and buildings, yet behind this is another world of organized satanic activity. We see forces of evil that pervade society and we think this is the problem. Divorce, addictions, genocide, euthanasia, pornography, teenage pregnancy, and many other damaging forces are evident. Yet there is a force of spiritual power energized by the devil and expedited by his minions that become the force behind the force. We see the system of democracy, autocracy, monarchy, dictatorship and we feel that these systems are flawed and produce problems. Yet behind this system there is another system of saturated iniquity, filled with the spirit of antichrist that infiltrates the systems that we see. The world that we see is permeated by the forces of satanic power that are unseen. Abnormal things become normal, deviant behavior becomes acceptable and in many cases preferred. The society is anesthetized so that hell has enlarged its borders. Marriage is an assaulted institution, love turns into vengeance and renegade passion exercises its godless options. What we see is only produced by the animation of the forces of the enemy and what I see with my physical eyes is not the enemy, so deliverance and transformation will not come from the picket line or the newspaper.

SPIRITUAL ENEMIES; PHYSICAL STRATEGIES

Spiritual enemies cannot be deterred and stopped with the institution of physical strategies and methods. One of the most subtle deceptions of the devil is the focusing of the Christian's efforts and attention on the wrong enemy. Satan camouflages himself, masters his motives, secludes his strategy, and places upon his operations a thick veneer of seduction. So many Christians are swallowed by the vortex of resentment to other believers, separation from the saints and have assumed positions of offense because of disagreement, and disillusionment. The answers to these divisions and dissensions do not originate with reason, logic and the intellectual acumen of man. Only heaven has the answer for a ravaged, ruined, pillaged people, and the God of heaven retains the sovereign right to dispatch spiritual enemies with the word of His power. There must be an ascent from this pulverized world and this ascent must lead me to the Lord of Lords. God would not transform me through the new birth and then leave me trapped by a system energized by the devil himself.

Deism teaches that God has created the world but has left it to the evolution of man's will and behavior. This is a damnable heresy that is absolutely bankrupt. God has not abdicated His throne, nor has He surrendered the right of ownership and occupation to the whims and fancies of the minions of satan. I am not left alone to deal with the temptations, oppressions, and depressions of the enemy who is daily striving to shift our gaze from heaven to earth.

THE UPWARD DRAFT

Distractions, detours, and discouragements all have the same source, the devil, and the same motive, which is the decimation of the hope and vision of the saint. If, by these oppressive attacks the heart of the believer becomes hardened and heavy, the emotions become pulverized and pummeled, the hope of the future becomes but a faded glory, then the downward spiral into ignominy has begun. There is a divine plan that has been given to provide the saint with an upward perspective. Worship allows me to shift gears from earth to heaven.

Worship gives me the ability to rise to my Father which is in heaven. When I worship, my circumstances do not leave me, I leave them and there is no prison that holds the worshipping saint in its claws of darkness. No cage can stop the heart and spirit from whisking its way to the throne of the Father.

> Psalm 24:3 states, *"Who shall ascend into the hill of the Lord? Or who shall stand in His holy place?"*

When life has thrown curves, circumstances have multiplied with oppression and voices of defeat, and depression scream at me, worship allows me to fall into the arms of my Lord.

A Release Of and a Release From

As worship is released from my heart and it ascends to the Father, there is a simultaneous release by the Lord, of circumstances on my life. When Paul and Silas worshipped in prison, the circumstance of bondage no longer dominated them. When Joshua fell on his face before the Captain of the Host in worship, the insurmountable challenge of Jericho no longer overwhelmed him.

When Jehoshaphat told the praisers to go before the army in worship, the challenge of the multiplied enemies no longer brought fear. My God-given ability to worship must not be annulled by the force of the circumstances around me. The method of operation of the devil has not changed and his plan is still the attempt to rivet the saint to rivalry, seduce his sanctity, confuse his conviction and overwhelm the Christian with earthiness.

THE TEMPTATIONS OF THE TEMPORAL

What moments of majesty have been forfeit because of the absorption with worldliness, the succumbing to the temptations of the temporal, and being possessed with the profanity of flesh indulgence. All these are the satanic attempts to confuse, conquer, and to determinately adjust the priority of heaven to earth. This is a compulsion that brings revulsion that gives propulsion that could lead to expulsion. The enemies plan is plain and predictable. He must create an upheaval around me to obstruct the glory within me. In a very real sense, what you see is what you get. My gaze must be fixed and my focus clear. My eyes must not be riveted <u>on what is around me but Who is above me.</u> The release of my worship to my God is the answer to the release of hell's hold on my life. Scripture abounds with instances where people worshipped the Lord in the midst of unmitigated chaos and miracles happened.

GENESIS 22
THE FIRST MENTION OF WORSHIP

The first mention of worship in the Bible is found in Genesis 22.

Genesis 22:1-5 states, *"And it came to pass after these things, that God did tempt Abraham, and said unto him, Abraham: and he said, Behold, here I am. And he said, Take now thy son, thine only son Isaac, whom thou lovest, and get thee into the land of Moriah; and offer him there for a burnt offering upon one of the mountains which I will tell thee of. And Abraham rose up early in the morning, and saddled his ass, and took two of his young men with him, and Isaac his son, and clave the wood for the burnt offering, and rose up, and went into the place of which God had told him. Then on the third day Abraham lifted up his eyes, and saw the place afar off. And Abraham said unto his young men, Abide ye here with the ass; and I and the lad will go yonder and worship, and come again to you."*

The picture is very clear and it is filled with the revelation of ascending worship. Abraham was about to ascend the hill and go to the place that God had ordained. Verse 5 said he was going up to worship. Worship never happens in the down, dejected place of depression and disdain. This is the place that the enemy has trapped so many and as long as surroundings seclude, and circumstances conquer, there will be no ascent. I serve notice to the enemy that I will no longer be summoned or sequestered in this lonely vale of complaint and confusion.

THE WILL AND WORSHIP

I have made a determination that I will ascend. In verse 5 Abraham said, *"I and the lad will go..."*. There are two vital points that must be followed here. First of all it is the free exercise of my will. I will go up. My will may be attacked, assaulted, and weakened but in the final analysis, I decide where my will goes. There are many times in the book of Psalms that the words, "I will praise", "I will worship", "I will bless the Lord", appear. The exercise of the will in worship is vital. Let us consider the connection between the will and the manifestation of the kingdom of God in us and around us.

> Matthew 6:10 states, *"Thy kingdom come. Thy will be done in earth, as it is in heaven."*

It is the will of God to be in me and around me and the key to the descent of the Kingdom is the ascent of the will. I will be dealing with the descent in a later chapter, but at this moment I will deal with the ascent of worship by your will. The greatest hindrance to the glory of the will of God, is the fleshly interruptions of the will of man. If the will of God is done, then the Kingdom of God is executed. The enemy must then infect the lives of men with this perpendicular pronoun called **I**. The middle letter of SIN is **I**, the prominent letter in PRIDE is **I,** and **I** is seen in the word LUCIPHER. The will, imbued with sin, weakened by the fall, and constantly biased to the repressive regime of self-centeredness must be turned around to be submitted to the Lord Jesus. The prolific exercise of a sin-centered will, is the foundation of deviant life. Now the time has come, by a conscious choice, a determined move, and a life rushing to the Father to say, "Not my will but Thine be done." Self-gratification, self-absorption, self-indulgence are only present because of the profane exercise of a sinful, flesh- possessed will. It is time to rise up and declare in the power of the Holy Spirit that my will is no longer under the domination of satan. Devil, your tenancy is over and your period of occupation has ended. If I do what I can, and God does what I can't, I have just entered the domain of the King and the Kingdom of God will become substantively mine.

OTHER MANIFESTATIONS OF THE KINGDOM

When the kingdom of God comes among us, there are several manifestations of glory that ensue. Let us examine some of those.

> Luke 11:20 states, *"But if I with the finger of God cast out devils, no doubt the kingdom of God is upon you."*

When the kingdom of God is manifested, there is the presence of deliverance, for demons have to flee from the presence of the King. The enemy, to perpetuate the presence of his principalities and powers, must do all he can to hinder the inauguration of the kingdom of God. His major tactic is to do all he can to trap men and women in the maze of self-centeredness and self-absorption.

Every tactic of the enemy is founded on the drive to exercise my will for selfish purposes.

Luke 10:9 states, *"And heal the sick that are therein, and say unto them, The kingdom of God is come nigh unto you."*

When the kingdom of God is executed, the sick are healed. This is not just limited to physical healing, but emotional, mental, and spiritual healing. If the enemy is to keep humanity in emotional dysfunction, mental instability, and spiritual darkness, he must cause the "I" life to be the most prominent. The will of man, when it is focused on nothing but self, becomes the breeding ground for every other evil. The devil is after the will and he will employ every gratifying, satiating tactic to ensure that life revolves around the "I" life.

THREEFOLD MANIFESTATIONS OF THE KINGDOM

Romans 14:17 gives a three-fold effect that the kingdom of God brings. It states, *"For the kingdom of God is not meat and drink; but righteousness, and peace, and joy in the Holy Ghost."*

Righteousness, peace, and joy are manifestations of the kingdom of God. Our world is saturated with unrighteousness and this is not only seen in what people do but what they are. Righteousness, is more than the act of being right. It involves equity in character and a spiritual balance between man and God. It's from this rightness, this equity, and this character that our relationships are blessed.

There is a level of wrongness and an absence of equity in character that has produced a non-caring, violent, and ambivalent society. Righteousness is a vital missing component in this flesh driven, "I" possessed culture.

Another manifestation of the kingdom of God is peace. This is not only peace with man, but the peace of God within man.

> James 4:1 states, *"From whence come wars and fightings among you? Come they not hence, even of your lusts that war in your members?"*

Nations do not go to war, people do. Warrings, whether they be familial, national, or international, are spawned from the same evil. These warrings begin within us and the only one who has access to the heart is Jesus Christ. If men were at peace with God, then peace would fill the inside and our relationships would be transformed. Our schools would ceaseto be war zones, our homes would cease to be centers of dysfunction, and our relationships would not be troubled by hostility.

JOY VS. HAPPINESS

When the kingdom of God descends there is joy. Happiness is decided by the things around you or the people around you so it is contingent on the external. Joy is dependent on nothing external for it is built on and given by God Himself. My relationship with my Lord produces my joy. External anomalies and life's riddles have no effect on my joy. The joy of the Lord is my strength so from the fountain of this joy comes strength. This is not a strength that is produced by performance, approval, or fleshly association. This strength flows from my Father which is in heaven. Just as sorrow and weakness are connected, so too joy and strength are connected.

> Hebrews 12:2 states, *"Looking unto Jesus the author and finisher of our faith; who for the joy that was set before him endured the cross, despising the shame, and is set down at the right hand of the throne of God."*

The cross was the most reprehensible death possible and the act of crucifixion was the mostpainful of deaths. Hands and feet pierced, His head crowned with thorns, His body emaciated, His back lacerated and furrowed by the whipping. Yet in the midst of this violent death that was painfully slow, Jesus saw the joy that was set before Him. Because He saw what He was going to, He was helped for what He was going through. This joy that enabled Him to see tomorrow, also empowered Him to wing His way past the horrific hurt, the scandalous shame, and the oppressive brutality. This is a joy that we all must understand and internalize for in the midst of our trial, suffering and pain though they pale into insignificance in the light of the cross, the joy will help us to be strong in the midst of chaos.

THE WILL AND THE KINGDOM

The exercise of my will as it is submitted to God opens the door for God's will to be unhindered in its execution. Now as I see these manifestations of the kingdom of God, deliverance, healing, righteousness, peace and joy, become the air I breathe. The subject of the "I" life is dealt with in detail in Romans 7:14-24. In ten verses, the word I is mentioned twenty four times. In Paul's description of his struggle, he did not mention the devil once. This is an ominous aspect to spiritual warfare because now it is internalized. The whole purpose of this godless infatuation with fleshly living is to eliminate the possibility of the manifestation of the kingdom of God. The exercise of the will in worship is the thing that leads to the ascent and the consequence is the descent of God's glory.

In Genesis 22:5 Abraham exercised his right to ascend and this determination had a direct connection to his son. As he ascended to the place of sacrifice which typifies the act of worship, he was able to take his son with him. This ascent had an effect on his family. If this determination to ascend is made, then the door is opened for a familial blessing as God begins to touch and restore.

> The same verse (Genesis 22:5) said, *"And I will come again to you."*

True worship guarantees a return of blessing and multiplication. Genesis 22:13 gives another wonderful consequence of the determined will that ascends.

> Genesis 22 verse 13 states, *"And Abraham lifted up his eyes, and looked, and behold behind him a ram caught in a thicket by his*

horns: and Abraham went and took the ram, and offered him up for a burnt offering in the stead of his son."

LIFT UP YOUR EYES, LOOK UP AND BEHOLD

On this mountain Abraham lifted up his eyes, he looked, and he beheld. This is a wonderful three-fold result of the focused, worshipful life. On this hill of worship, he was able to lift up his eyes. In the place of worship, the vision is celestial. All challenges and struggles pale into oblivion. Here he was preparing the altar to place the one son that he loved so deeply. As he is about to plunge the knife into the son who was the son of promise, he was stopped. Sometimes you have to sacrifice what you love the most to get what you need the most.

This text on worship, Genesis 22, involves some of the greatest insight on worship in the entire Bible. On this mountain, his vision was upward so he could look and behold. In these moments of ascent in worship, eyes are filled with inspiration, illumination and revelation. On this mountain of ascent an astonishing revelation of God is given. It is here that the name Jehovah Jireh is given. The Lord is my provider. This name of God has had eternal effects on God's people throughout the ages and they have gleanedencouragement, edification, and hope from this precious name. This name was given as God's response to His servant who ascended a hill to worship. Worship as an ascent is one of the most pivotal truths in the Bible, and from it there is a spiritual universe of unmatched revelation that emerges.

LEFT IN THE VALLEY

Genesis 22:5 gives another point that is paramount to the ascent.

> Genesis 22 verse 5 states, *"And Abraham said unto his young men, abide ye here with the ass: and I and the lad will go yonder and worship, and come again to you."*

The two young men that helped them on the journey had to stay at the bottom of the mountain. Before the ascent to worship there are always things that must be left behind. The reason why so many still remain at the bottom of the mountain and have been unable to ascend is because of their unwillingness to leave behind the things that are fleeting. These young men fulfilled their purpose in helping Abraham and Isaac to get here. Now it was time to go up but the ascent had to be preceded by a separation.

When worship is studied, this aspect of ascent is obvious. What is not as obvious is what the ascent leads to. If I ascend in worship, what then is God's response? As we continue to walk through this revelation, be prepared to experience a dimension of God's operation that you may have never experienced before. Never in scripture did someone long for God with fervor, separate himself/herself to get to where God is, without a providential interposition and a divine visitation. There are things that must be left in the lonely valley that must not accompany you in your ascent. I must not be weighed down in the valley with baggage so that I cannot begin my ascent to the Father. The heaven later, power later, blessing later theology is not the message that resounds today. My battlefield is here on planet earth and my need for Heaven's touch is desperate. There is much that God has to offer and I don't have to wait until the Millennium reign is inaugurated to experience these blessings. God is waiting for a group of people to wing their way to Him in ascent and worship. His response is the descent of His presence and His companionship as He walks among us.

CHAPTER 1

SUMMARY

1. Worship is ascent into the presence of God.
2. The world is a system, and a force energized by the power of the enemy.
3. When I enter into worship, my circumstances don't leave me, I leave them in a holy ascent.
4. This ascent is a release of my spirit and a release from the things that bind.
5. Genesis 22 brings the first illustration of worship in the Bible.
6. This chapter gives two major principles in Genesis 22:5. Abraham exercised his will to ascend and took his son with him.
7. The will of man is the greatest obstacle to the will of God.
8. The will of God when it is executed brings the blessings of the kingdom of God.
9. Deliverance, healing, righteousness, peace and joy are all manifestations of the kingdom of God.
10. The ascent in worship is a principle that is preparation for the descent of power.

Chapter 2

Heaven Reached: Earth Touched

Matthew 6:9 states, *"After this manner therefore pray ye: Our Father which art in heaven, Hallowed be thy name."*

This ascent to the heavenly realm is emphasized in the first verse of this immortal prayer. This is more than a recommended prayer or a liturgical exercise of suggested repetition. This is a life giving principle that ushers the worshipper into the very presence of God. There are many revolutionary spiritual insights given in Matthew 6:9-13. The coming of the kingdom of God, the will of God, the giving of daily bread, forgiveness to others, deliverance from evil, are some of the pristine doctrines given in this text. But here is the point of revelation and exclamation.

All of this begins with verse 9, which states, *"Our Father which art in heaven,"* Before earth can be touched, transformed, exhibit triumph, Heaven must be seen, and sought after. The miracle of all that happens in verses 10-13 is predicated on an upward gaze to heaven. It is an ascent. The recognition of heaven's power gives the ability to be loosed from earth's prisons. This glorious life will only begin as we ascend and this upward look takes us past earthly restraints.

Jacob's Ladder

Jacob received a life-changing experience that would be the foundation to which he would return on repeated occasions. This place would become his sanctuary, and in times of trauma, it represented the place of transformation and triumph over turmoil. This experience began with a ladder. This ladder provided the possibility of an ascent.

Genesis 28:12-13 states, *"And he dreamed, and behold a ladder set up on the earth, and the top of it reached to heaven: and behold the angels of God ascending and descending on it. And, behold, the Lord stood above it, and said, I am the Lord God of Abraham thy father, and the God of Isaac: the land whereon thou liest, to thee will I give it, and to thy seed;"*

As this ladder took the climber to heaven, the glorious object of the ascent was to touch the Lord.

Chapter 13:1 declares, *"And the Lord stood above it"*.

This is a statement that is replete with inspiration and revelation. Let us examine some pivotal pointers that are given by these six words.

1. When I ascend this ladder, there is no detour or deviation.
2. In my ascent, enemies that are energized by the worldly spirit are impotent to hinder me.
3. The destiny of this holy traveler is fixed.
4. When I ascend in prayer, praise, and worship, the Lord is above me.
5. If the Lord is above, all the traumas and trials of earth are below.
6. It is in seeing this superintending sovereignty of my Lord that I find my most profound provision.
7. I am not shackled by surroundings or enveloped by environment because in my ascent, I am free.
8. Whatever the force of the enemy is, it is my determination to climb this ladder.
9. As the Lord stands above the ladder, the arrival of the saint brings an inheritance to the climber.

10. The ascent to meet the Lord is only preparatory for the miracle of the descent.

SIGHT + STORM + WAVES = FEAR

The method of operation of the devil is very predictable and there is an abundance of revelation in the Old and New Testament that unmasks his pathetic strategy. The devil's vilest attack on the saint is to keep his vision earthward, his mind zeroed in on circumstance, and his heart swallowed with fear. This apparently oversimplistic strategy has been the undoing of many lives.

> This is graphically illustrated in Matthew 14:29-31, *"And He said, Come. And when Peter was come down out of the ship, he walked on the water, to go to Jesus. But when he saw the wind boisterous, he was afraid; and beginning to sink, he cried, saying, Lord, save me. And immediately Jesus stretched forth his hand, and caught him, and said unto him, O thou of little faith, wherefore didst thou doubt?"*

Let us examine this text. In the midst of the storm, with rising waves, and a reeling ship Peter was summoned by the Lord's word, "Come". The sea, the waves, the reeling and rocking, the threatening circumstance and the forbidding foment were absolutely irrelevant. Peter had the power of the word, come. He came out of the boat, and walked on the water; so Peter must not be criticized for failing. He came out of the boat while the others languished and for moments, he walked on the thing that was his source of oppression and fear. This is worthy of commendation. You can walk on the thing that has caused your fear as you follow the word of the Lord. However, attacks of the enemy come. Verse 30 begins, *"But when he saw."* Here is the primary temptation of the enemy and it is as age old as the garden of Eden.

> Genesis 3:6 states, *"And when the woman saw that the tree was good for food, and that it was pleasant to the eyes, and a tree to be desired to make one wise, she took of the fruit thereof, and did eat, and gave also unto her husband with her; and he did eat."*

WHAT YOU SEE IS WHAT YOU GET

Here is the attack in the beginning. *"And the woman saw"*. It is the purpose of the enemy to open the eyes to that which is forbidden. One of the three attacks of the flesh is the lust of the eyes so when the fleshy gaze is fixed, the carnal maze begins. The fleshly gaze introduces the carnal maze and life is razed. Temptation comes at the point of limitation and the enemy's workshop is to get the eyes to be focused on the forbidden. Peter's demise began when he saw. He saw the wind boisterous. What he saw became the source of his demise and when he saw it, it was boisterous, eruptive, and dangerous. The enemy will ensure that what you see is so obviously dangerous that your entire life will be derailed from God's holy purpose.

There are many that state that what you say is what you get, but here it was what you see is what you get. The quality or lack of quality of the life I live is directly contingent on the vision and focus of my eyes. It is obvious that the wind is invisible, but the effects of the wind on the sea created a boisterous condition. Satan causes upheaval in the things around us and his ultimate aim is to cause us to fall by dwelling on the visible. The next thing that happened after he saw the wind was the emotion of fear. Sight added to circumstance-created fear. The Bible then states in verse 30 that he began to sink and this sinking was a product of what he saw. When my gaze is purposefully fixed on Jesus, there is no circumstance that can bury me. I am determined not to be deterred because of undisciplined sight. I have decided without equivocation to have my eyes fixed on the Lord.

EYES LIFTED - LIFE GIFTED

In Genesis 22:4 it states, *"Then on the third day Abraham lifted up his eyes, and saw the place afar off."*

Abraham lifted up his eyes and placed his sight on the place that God wanted him to be. Whenever the eyes are fixed on what God desires, there will be a vision of the place of provision. A vision of provision is only given to those who lift up their eyes. Verse 5 speaks of the ascent of the mountain to the place where God would supernaturally provide a ram.

Verse 13 states, *"And Abraham lifted up his eyes, and looked, and behold behind him a ram caught in a thicket by his horns: and Abraham went and took the ram, and offered him up for a burnt offering in the stead of his son."*

Once again Abraham lifted up his eyes and saw God's sovereign provision of the ram. This is the holy sequence. Lift up your eyes, ascend to the place of providence and provision, and see the glory of the God who will provide.

LEFT BEHIND ALONE IN THE VALLEY

Genesis 22:5 states, *"And Abraham said unto his young men, Abide ye here with the ass; and I and the lad will go yonder and worship, and come again to you."*

This is a very significant thought in relation to the ascent of worship. The lads that came to this point with him were not able to make the trip to the place of provision. There will be things that are left in the valley when the ascent begins. This ascent is a very personal thing that will create very personal consequences and things that are peripheral must be left in the valley. Abraham becomes a prototype, not only of the faith life, but the worship experience.

There is another pivotal pointer on worship that will be dealt with in a later chapter concerning Abraham's experience on Mount Moriah. The word Moriah means the fear of the Lord. This is the thing that is so absent in the church today, and its absence speaks of the weakness in the approach to worship. This miracle of Genesis 22:13 did not take place in the valley with the lads, but it took place on the mountain after ascent. God is calling His people to a higher experience, and the things that may have accompanied you to this point are not the things that you ascend with. So many have become saturated with a system that they forget the Son. It is never about what surrounds you, but it is about the Son who is within you.

It is the ascent to worship that disconnects you from the familiarity with the system and allows you to revel in the "SONSHINE". I have dwelt on the ascent for a while because it is of vital importance to understand that gloomy things happen in the prison of circumstance in the low place. Your ascent is the conscious exercise of the will and whether the will is weakened, oppressed, or prejudiced to carnality, you can and must ascend.

Father Knows Best

Isaac was the son of promise and the hopes of a father and a nation were consummated in this son. The name Isaac means laughter, and this was the true feeling of a pleased father to know that this promised son would be the perpetuator of the covenant. It was this son that would be taken to the mountain, by the conscious will of the father. There was nothing subliminal or subconscious about this act. The willingness to stay in the low place is an act of the will. With this understanding, I exercise my divinely given prerogative to declare, I will ascend. He was willing to give up what he loved the most and was about to receive what he needed the most. Obedience must include the surrender of the things that are dearly treasured and closely protected. There was no negotiation by Isaac as to whether he was willing to go, because he was under the authority of his father, so he was obligated to follow the order of Abraham. These things that are loved, that must be surrendered must not be given a bargaining position.

> Genesis 22:5 states, *"And Abraham said unto his young men, Abide ye here with the ass; and I and the lad will go yonder and worship, and come again to you."*

The lad and I will go. I speak for the things that are under my authority. You will go up. We will ascend. There will be a surrender. I will worship.

Chapter 2

Summary

1. The prayer of Matthew 6 begins with worship. "Our Father which art in heaven."
2. Jacob's ladder illustrates the possibility of the ascent of worship and the descent of blessings.
3. The operation of the devil always deals with sight plus storm plus waves that bring fear.
4. In a very real way, what you see is what you get.
5. In Genesis 22:4, Abraham lifted up his eyes. Eyes are lifted, life is gifted.
6. When the ascent of worship is made, there are things left behind in the valley.
7. The Mount of worship that Abraham ascended is Moriah which means the fear of God.
8. When Abraham took what he loved the most, Isaac, he received what he needed the most, a potential father to Israel.

Chapter 3

The Crucified I

Romans 7 is the preeminent chapter in the Bible that identifies the subtle infiltrator called "I". This intransigent traitor, this selfish bigot, this fleshly fiend is at the source of the battle for survival in the Christian life. Paul is giving an astonishing revelation concerning the battle he is having. In Romans 7:16-21, not once is the word demon, devil, or principality used. However, the word I is used twenty two times. There are three enemies that confront the believer on a daily basis. The world is the external enemy, the devil is the infernal enemy, and the flesh is the internal enemy. The world or the devil is powerless to do anything in the believer if the flesh, the internal enemy, is crucified and dead.

Obsession, depression, and regression take place when the internal enemy, the flesh, is uncrucified and then invites fellowship with the world and the devil. This "I" life, the flesh, is the fountainhead of evil and when this flesh is crucified, the will of man is freed and liberated to realms of glory. Fleshly saturation obstructs spirit exaltation. The strategy of the enemy is to create a blockade in my inner man to be sure that there is no ascent in worship. His most demented work is done in a flesh filled, carnally conquered life.

Galations 2:20 states, *"I am crucified with Christ: nevertheless I live; yet not I, but Christ liveth in me: and the life of which I now live in the flesh, I live by the faith of the Son of God, who loved me, and gave Himself for me."*

THE EXCHANGED LIFE

It is not I but Christ. This is the exchanged life for I crucify my "I" and I bow to Jesus. In the low place of compromise, disobedience, and unwillingness, I am drawn into the vortex of sin and flesh that swirls my life around in an unholy whirlwind. It is the arrogance and presumption of a renegade life that creates destruction in my life. When the center of gravity ceases to be "I" and it becomes Jesus, then the ascent has begun. Presumption brings consumption, but exaltation brings glorification. I exalt the name of Jesus because I have placed my name in the place of death. There is heavenly manifestation awaiting the ascender, as my will is placed in the upward direction.

The name of God can only be glorified if the name of man is crucified. So many seek arduously and diligently to protect this name, which represents a glorying in fleshly accomplishment and the achievement of personal ambition.

II Chronicles 7:14 states, *"If My people, which are called by My name, shall humble themselves, and pray, and seek My face, and turn from their wicked ways; then will I hear from Heaven, and will forgive their sin, and will heal their land."*

When my life is given to Christ I am called by the name of God. True worship is the exaltation of the name of God, and the defamation of my personal fleshly nature.

THE THREE IMPOSTORS

The internal enemy called the flesh is the catalyst for conquest, the reason for ruin, and the seducer of the saved. It thrives on the camouflage of appetites, and it spawns a series of subtleties that surround the saint and saturate the soul. Life then becomes an abhorrent manifestation of spiritual bankruptcy, and this fraudulent supercheater called flesh now opens the door to shameful apostasy. It is possible to render this slothful, scandalous traitor powerless as is profoundly exhibited in the life of our Lord.

John 14:30 states, *"Hereafter I will not talk much with you: for the prince of this world cometh, and hath nothing in Me."*

The prince of the world came and found nothing in Jesus, and the devil was unable to proceed with his diabolical purpose. Consider the three fold implication and co-operation between this unholy alliance. The prince of the world, the devil is enemy number one, being the source and the evil fountain head of all licentious experience. He is not just a prince, but the prince of the world, so even though he is the source of this evil he must have a channel of expression. The world becomes this renegade realm that is the repository for all the profanity and brutality of the devil himself. The world, because of its propensity to sin and selfishness, with its biased behavior to rebellion and treachery now authorizes the devil to be its master.

HE FOUND NOTHING IN ME

Verse 30 gives a powerful revelation concerning the ultimate purpose of these fiends when it says that, *"he found nothing in Me"*. The purpose was to bring the source and the realm, who are the devil and the world, into the life of Jesus.

Even though the devil and the world are filled with destructive potential and venomous tactics, there must be an entry point, a bridgehead that allows these external forces to be internalized. Satan's power to deceive, darken and destroy is impotent unless he finds the internal imposter, the flesh, to be kind and co-operative. It is here that the words of verse 30 provides illumination that rings through the ages and the passage of time will never reduce its awesome impact. He found nothing in me.

When lives are filled and flooded with flesh-focused feelings, the devil's external temptation and taunting finds internal acceptance and approval. When this inside imposter is left uncrucified, it produces an overpowering passion for sinful indulgence. It produces an enormous appetite for carnality and worldliness, and it becomes an abysmal, bottomless pit that has no satisfaction until it completely mutilates the life it possesses.

TRUE WORSHIP VS. FALSE WORSHIP

Just as true worship to my Father exudes from my spirit, the false worship of the flesh on the inside gushes out to the father of all sinful experience, who is the devil. My spirit on the inside is excited and ready to launch itself into true worship, and my flesh on the inside is ready to attempt to abort this holy worship by the exercise of unholy flesh. It is mandatory that we understand that the uncrucified "I" is the attempt of the enemy to detour, deter, and discourage my worship to my Father. The aim of the flesh is to smother men beneath its evil, religious, bigoted, carnal cloak and replace the worship of God with the worship of self. If it is possible for Jesus, in his human condition, to live in the place where the devil found nothing in Him, then that same testimony can be mine today. No external power, temptation, or invasion can affect me if my flesh is crucified, and my inside is submitted to the will of the Father. I am not advocating that life will be resplendent and perfect, but I am saying that my inside will not be puppeteered and dominated by the strings of temptation. The enemy and his power will not decide the quality of my spiritual life nor will he produce the air that I breathe. My inner peace will not be penetrated by outer conflict. It is very important to know that this realm of resistance, this power and purpose, this inner protection and preservation is available! So that when the devil comes, he will find nothing in you.

I Will Return

This powerful possibility is seen in graphic description in Luke 4:3-13,

> Luke 4:3-13 *"And the devil said unto him, If thou be the Son of God, command this stone that it be made bread. And Jesus answered him, saying, It is written, That man shall not live by bread alone, but by every word of God. And the devil, taking him up into an high mountain, shewed unto him all the kingdoms of the world in a moment of time. And the devil said unto him, All this power will I give thee, and the glory of them: for that is delivered unto me; and to whomsoever I will I give it. If thou therefore wilt worship me, all shall be thine. And Jesus answered and said unto him, Get thee behind me, satan: for it is written, Thou shalt worship the Lord thy God, and Him only shalt thou serve. And he brought Him to Jerusalem, and set Him on a pinnacle of the temple, and said*

unto Him, If Thou be the Son of God, cast Thyself down from hence: For it is written, He shall give His angels charge over thee, to keep thee: And in their hands they shall bear thee up, lest at any time thou dash thy foot against a stone. And Jesus answering said unto him, It is said, Thou shalt not tempt the Lord thy God. And when the devil had ended all the temptation, he departed from Him for a season."

Verse 13 states that the devil departed from Jesus for a season, and verse 14 declares that Jesus returned in the power of the Spirit into Galilee and fame of Him went through the region. Now think of this for a moment. Whatever happened in the wilderness, regardless of how potent the problem, or how howling the wilderness and concentrated the temptation, Jesus won.

After the temptation, He returned in the power of the Spirit and fame of His power spread through all the region. This is the place we ultimately want to be. Where we return from temptation, but we return in the power of the Spirit, so that the fame of Jesus spreads through the region. When temptation is dispatched from the devil like a flood, the purpose is to consume you to the point where there is no possibility of return, the point of no return. However, Jesus' victory in the midst of temptation guarantees the possibility of my return. The return in the power of the Spirit precludes the effort of the flesh to weaken and defeat me. Now Jesus is glorified as He returns in power, and the entire region is impacted by His presence. Something happened in the wilderness temptation that brought Jesus out and now because of this victory, we have an example of power.

TEMPTATION ONE

The experience in the wilderness with temptation emerges with astonishing implications for our present conflicts and has great truths that apply to this worship, When God Walks Among Us theme.

Luke 4:2-4 declares, *"Being forty days tempted of the devil. And in those days He did eat nothing: and when they were ended, He afterward hungered. And the devil said unto Him, If thou be the Son of God, command this stone that it be made bread. And Jesus answered him, saying, It is written, That man shall not live by bread alone, but by every word of God."*

In a time of fasting, physical weakness and hunger, this profane predator, the devil, comes to overwhelm Jesus with the temptation to turn the stone to bread. Jesus' response to this attack was simple yet profound, immediate yet with eternal results, for His temptation, was to set an example for all temptation. Jesus' method in dealing with this temptation was, *"It is written. Man shall not live by bread alone, but by every word of God."*

There was no invitation for angels to participate, no union of holy men, or agreement of partners in prayer; it was the simple statement that it was written.

> And so it was written as Deuteronomy 8:3 states, *"And He humbled thee, and suffered thee to hunger, and fed thee with manna, which thou knewest not, neither did thy fathers know; that He might make thee know man doth not live by bread only, but by every word that proceedeth out of the mouth of the Lord doth man live."*

Jesus went back to the Old Testament and chose one of the verses of the Torah to defeat the enemy in His time of intense battle. I believe that the reason this was done is to emphasize and confirm that this same word with all its dynamism, power, and explosiveness is available to the believer today.

TEMPTATION TWO

Verses 5 – 8 give the second temptation and this temptation deals with the second aspect of the operation of the flesh, the lust of the eyes. Jesus was taken to a high mountain and was asked by the devil to see all the kingdoms. This was the attempt to cause Jesus to submit because of what He saw and was offered. The devil offered Jesus the power and glory of these kingdoms and he was convinced that Jesus would capitulate and surrender to this temptation.

Verse 7 states, *"If thou therefore wilt worship me, all shall be thine."*

This is where this text is connected to the theme of this book, for in the seduction and deception of the devil, he endeavors to create a form of duplicate worship.

LUCIFER'S "I WILLS"

Isaiah 14: 13, 14 states, *"For thou hast said in thine heart, I will ascend into heaven, I will exalt my throne above the stars of God: I will sit also upon the mount of the congregation, in the sides of the north: I will ascend above the heights of the clouds; I will be like the Most High."*

This presents the five "I wills" that filled the heart of Lucifer that precipitated his demise. This "I" possession is the poison that vanquishes the mighty and with burning indignation robs us of divine purpose. This is not the place to deal with the five "I wills" but we must consider with a cursory look, the last two. Verse 13 speaks about sitting upon the mount of the congregation in the sides of the north. Lucifer's' determination was to sit upon the mount of the congregation. This could have been the place where the angels assembled to worship the Lord, and this is the place that Lucifer wanted to occupy.

This was the desire that began the demise of Lucifer and created the person we see today as the diabolical devil. This fall was preceded by the "I will" that led to the desire for worship. The "I" life, the renegade uncontrolled exercise of fleshliness is only the attempt of the soul to demand a duplicate worship that creates a fall.

Going back to Luke 4:7, this worship was tied to the giving of the power and the glory of the kingdoms of the world. This is the subtle infiltrator that demands a bowed knee, a bent life, and promises that the world will give to you its power and glory.

THE LAST I WILL

The second "I will" in Isaiah 14:14 was that Lucifer wanted to ascend above the heights of the clouds and he declared like a usurper, I will be like the Most High. The clouds are always associated to the glory of God, so Lucifer wanted to ascend above this glory. Along with this, he wanted to be like the most high God. God was and is worshipped for He alone is worthy of this adoration and adulation. From this perspective Lucifer was not content to be a reflection, he wanted to be the light. In simple terms, he wanted the throne, the glory, and he wanted to be God. The original absorption with the "I life" took place with Lucifer, and it led to the attempt to usurp the throne of God and take God's place.

Since that moment in eternity past, even before creation began in Genesis, when the devil was kicked out of heaven, the true worship of the saints to the God of Heaven has been and is a constant reminder of his failure and doom. We are giving to God the very thing that Lucifer was kicked out of heaven for endeavoring to receive. So sanctified saint, worshipping warrior, keep the praises and the worship going up! Glorify God and decimate the devil.

THE THIRD TEMPTATION

Luke 4:9-12 speaks of the third temptation and this temptation was related to the pride of life. Satan brought Jesus to the pinnacle of a temple and said, If You be the Son of God, cast Thyself down from hence for it is written, He shall give His angels charge over thee to keep thee and in their hands they shall bear thee up, lest at any time thou dash thy foot against a stone. The devil quoted this scripture from Psalms 91:11, 12 and of course, true to his nature, he misquoted the verse. He was tempting Jesus to take the arrogant position of independence and through the razzle dazzle of His position, cast Himself down, and He would be protected anyway.

A PERFECT TRACK RECORD BROKEN

All these temptations were centered on eliciting from Jesus a fleshly response, so that the result would be the worship of satan and the perpetuation of the fleshly parade. Consider this thought for a moment. All through the Old Testament, with all the patriarchs, the kings, prophets, and priests, there was some moment in their lives where fleshly indulgence was recorded. When the devil came to Jesus with these temptations, his unholy track record of defeating the lives of the holy was astonishing. With this, he confronts Jesus and for the first time since his attacks on humanity, the devil finds someone who will not bow, who cannot be bought, who is what He says He is. It must have been a moment when the devil's plot was pulverized and pummeled. Jesus with thunder in His voice and tempest in His brow sent a message that resounded in the ranks of the oppressors that is still reverberating today, "IT IS WRITTEN".

It is now within my capability to deal with this internal imposter, this fleshly fiend in my inner man, because the same word that was accessible to Jesus is accessible to me. If the "I" life, because of its versatility and deception, chooses to faint, or fake, or fool, then life will be filled with deception and duplicity. This "I" of the soul must be crucified so that the Christ in my spirit can be glorified.

Please remember that the saturation of "I" will do what I want, when I want, how I want, and nobody can tell me what to do attitude is a reproduction of a Luciferic position that got him kicked out of Heaven. I must do nothing to perpetuate the lie of this venomous villain, this possessed perpetrator called the devil.

Chapter 3

Summary

1. Romans 7 is the preeminent chapter in the Bible that identifies the "I" life.
2. The three enemies are the world, the flesh, and the devil.
3. External temptation must have internal invitation.
4. It is possible to live a crucified life so that the devil finds nothing in you.
5. The three temptations of Jesus represent the lust of the flesh, the lust of the eyes, and the pride of life.
6. If Jesus conquered these temptations by the "IT IS WRITTEN" revelation, so can we.
7. Isaiah 14 gives the five "I wills" of Lucifer.

Chapter 4

When God Walks Among Us

One of the pervasive truths that is woven in the fabric of scripture from Genesis to The Revelation, is God's desire to walk among His people. This is an element and aspect of God's operation that has not been given the recognition it deserves. We all speak with great rhetoric about earth's approach to Heaven but the same emphasis needs to be given to Heaven's approach to earth. What I do for God is predicated on what God has done for me. The purposes that direct my life on earth are only fructified by heaven's purposes for my life.

There is a unique heavenly presence that is transformed from God's domain in Heaven to my life.

> Genesis 3:8 and Revelation 21:3 state, *"And they heard the voice of the Lord God walking in the garden in the cool of the day: and Adam and his wife hid themselves from the presence of the Lord God amongst the trees of the garden."*

"And I heard a great voice out of heaven saying, Behold, the tabernacle of God is with men, and He will dwell with them, and they shall be His people, and God Himself shall be with them, and be their God."

GOD'S PRESENCE, PRESERVATION, AND POWER

God's plan includes, not just the blessing of the saints with specific interventions and breakthroughs, but it includes the protection, preservation and power of His perpetual presence among us and around us. In Genesis, God walked among them and with them. In the book of Revelation, He tabernacles and dwells among His people. There is a divine enlargement and enrichment when my faith receives the revelation that God is dwelling with me and walks among His people. The devil has no power to retort and his only option is to retreat. This concept begins in the book of Genesis and it will never be terminated because it continues in the New Jerusalem.

Moses crystallizes this thought with unerring accuracy in Exodus 33:15,

Exodus 33:15 *"And he said unto Him, If Thy presence go not with me, carry us not up hence."*

Moses is about to receive the second covenant (law) because the first tablets of the law were broken because of the sin of the people. He is asking the Lord to go with him and if God will not go, Moses refuses to move. Lord, let your presence go with us, and walk with me. There is an astonishing explanation given as to why Moses is adamant about God's presence being with him.

> Exodus 33:16 states, *"For wherein shall it be known here that I and Thy people have found grace in Thy sight? Is it not in that Thou goest with us? So shall we be separated, I and Thy people, from all the people that are upon the face of the earth."*

If You walk with us, among us, and Your presence goes with us, it will be known by all that we have found grace and favor in Your sight. There is a spiritual transfiguration that takes place when I know that God is walking amongst the affairs of my life. Grace and favor are only consequences of this wonderful august presence, and when God walks among His people, His face is seen.

WALKING AMONG THE CANDLESTICKS

Revelation 1:12, 13 declares, *"And I turned to see the voice that spake with me. And being turned, I saw seven golden candlesticks; And in the midst of the seven candlesticks one like unto the Son of man, clothed with a garment down to the foot, and girt about the paps with a golden girdle."*

These seven golden candlesticks or lampstands are of great importance for in verse 20 these lampstands represent the seven churches. These lampstands were seen in the Tabernacle and in the temple. The purpose of these lampstands was the distribution and the dissemination of light. This is a very appropriate parallel to the body of Christ, the church of the Lord Jesus that is called to show forth the light of God. When Jesus walked the earth in His flesh, He told the disciples that He was the light of the world, and as He walked with them, and they saw this light.

John 8:12; 9:5 declares, *"Then spake Jesus again unto them, saying, I am the light of the world: he that followeth me shall not walk in darkness, but shall have the light of life."* "As *long as I am in the world, I am the light of the world."*

When Jesus knew that his departure was nigh, He spoke to His disciples about His leaving, their responsibility, and an impartation to and a transfiguration of their lives.

Matthew 5:14 declares, *"Ye are the light of the world. A city that is set on an hill cannot be hid."*

Now, His word of power and transformation to them was that they are the light of the world. They became what Jesus was while He was with them by association, absorption, and impartation. The lampstands of the Tabernacle and the temple, had to be filled with oil to produce light. So too the church must be filled with the Holy Spirit to produce the light of God. There are so many in the realm of church life that are benighted by the darkness of religion, tradition, liturgy, and bigotry. There is no operation of the Holy Spirit so there is no production of light.

As the union begins to unfold, John sees someone like the Son of man walking in the midst of the candlesticks. What a magnificent picture of God walking among us.

Matthew 16:18 declares, *"And I say also unto thee, That thou art Peter, and upon this rock I will build My church; and the gates of hell shall not prevail against it."*

Jesus said this is My church, and it is Mine by right, by possession, by inheritance, and by foundation. Now the illustration is replete with revelation as the Son of man is in the midst of the lampstands or the churches. Here, He is called the Son of man and this reference is only given one more time in the Book of Revelation. As the Son of man, He identifies completely with the human condition, the feeling of our infirmity, the pain and the passion, and He is now ready to reach out with healing in His nail pierced hands.

There are many powerful points that must be considered concerning the Son of man being in the midst of the lampstands.

1. He is not separated and secluded from the needs of His people, He walks in the midst of them.
2. No force, power, oppressive brutality or satanic strategy will stop Him from walking in the midst of His own.
3. By walking among them, He inspects their

lives and work because He has an active interest.
4. By coming in, He establishes His sovereign right to be bigger than all that assails them.
5. In coming in the midst, He infuses them with His holy touch, hope, and power.
6. By being in the midst, He becomes the protector and preserver of the people.

As God walks among His people, there is a warning served to every minion of the devil, to every destructive plot that is engineered by satan, and that is: "These people whom I walk among are under divine scrutiny, divine occupation, and divine protection." Hallelujah!!! While there is failure and frustration, trepidation and trauma, death and destruction in the religious people around, here, in the place where the Son of man walks, Heaven's power and purpose are portrayed. It becomes an oasis in the desert, and a place where living waters flow.

I will not exclude my self from a sovereign move because of religious resistance for my heart, my life, my family longs to have the experience of God walking among us. Let the church be the church, let the righteous be the righteous, let the holy be the holy. This is who we are, and we will not be diluted into compromise. We are not a collection of saints waiting for the next bus ride to Heaven nor are we spiritless, anemic, and redundant. We are created for connection and destined for deliverance. The Son of man is in the midst of us, and it is our honor to recognize Him, love Him, and honor Him for who He is.

THE STARS IN HIS RIGHT HAND

Revelation 1:16 says, *"And He had in His right hand seven stars: and out of His mouth went a sharp two-edged sword: and His countenance was as the sun shineth in His strength."*

We know that the candlesticks are the churches and the stars are interpreted in verse 20. The stars are the angels, the ministers, or the messengers of these churches. God not only has a powerful plan for the corporate church, He also has a powerful plan for the ministers that lead these churches. There is a spiritually incensed world of pain and horror that satan has explosively launched against those who lead.

Satan desires to relegate redeemed leadership to a place of ruin, so he churns out his prodigious attacks that have intensified to magnum force in the past several months. In this zero hour, satan's role is to create overpowering passion in the lives of leadership to challenge the whole fabric of Spirit ordered church life. At times, the prevalence of these assaults seems to be within a hair's breadth of completely disintegrating leadership. But in these moments

God will not allow satan's strategy to succeed, and leadership no matter how crushed and conquered will rise to regain the glory that was taken.

The revelation of Jesus to the churches was that He was walking among them, but to the ministers, He held them in His right hand. This holding denotes possession with purpose. This is a heavenly initiative taken by Jesus Himself where He chooses to hold His servants, and He holds them in His right hand. The right hand is symbolic of authority and power. Jesus is seated at the right hand of the Father and this position establishes indisputable authority. His authority covers His servants so no man can pluck them out of His hands. The attempts of the enemy to take the joy, peace, righteousness, and power from the minister's life is met with the heavenly position of authority.

Today's ministry is smothered beneath a cloak of oppression, and excitement, and dynamism is extracted from so many servants, and the spiritual life becomes degraded and compromised. In these moments, God will manifest the power of His right hand to bless, to govern, and to execute judgment, and to those who will follow Him fully, these attacks will be made fleeting shadows. The purpose of the churches is to be holy conveyers or emitters of the light, and the leaders of the churches are to project the light into a dark and dying world.

To the church, He walked among them; to the ministers, He held them in his right hand. Holding in the right hand meant that He protected them by His authority and power. Walking among the churches meant He created His presence around them. We desperately stand in dire need of His protection and power and His presence.

GOD'S FACE – GOD'S HAND

The supplicating saint wants to see the demonstration of God's hand when God's interest is showing His face. If we seek the face of God, we will see the hand of God.

> II Chronicles 7:14 states, *"If My people, which are called by My name, shall humble themselves, and pray, and seek My face, and turn from their wicked ways; then will I hear*

from Heaven, and will forgive their sin, and will heal their land."

One of the greatest hindrances to seeking and seeing the face of God is the intrusion of the face of man. This is graphically illustrated in the celestial scene of,

> Isaiah 6:2, *"Above it stood the seraphims: each one had six wings; with twain he covered his face, and with twain he covered his feet, and with twain he did fly."*

The seraphim, who are around the throne, hid their face in the presence of God. Even though they are closest to and most familiar with this heavenly throne, they hid their face. We must adopt the same attitude.

I Hide My Face, So the Face of God Can Be Seen

> Leviticus 10:1,2 states, *"And Nadab and Abihu, the sons of Aaron, took either of them his censer, and put fire therein, and put incense thereon, and offered strange fire before the Lord, which He commanded them not. And*

there went out fire from the Lord, and devoured them, and they died before the Lord."

Nadab and Abihu had no right to offer sacrifices at the altar, but because of their connection to Aaron, they usurped a position, committed an extreme violation of God's word – and died in the presence of God. This exemplifies the constant peril of undue familiarity with divine things.

What these men offered to God in rebellion was called strange fire. It was offered in the temple but was not accepted by God. In fact it brought judgment on their lives. In the presence of God, they did not consider that only the face of God must be seen. It is for His glory and His honor, so they died in the place that was created to give life. There are many in the realm of church life who have become unduly familiar with divine things. Even though they have had constant exposure to the Son, they have not exposed themselves to the Son. They have hidden from Jesus what belongs to Him. Nadab and Abihu were sons of the priest but died a lonely death. May we never become so full of God that we don't need Him, and may we never be so close that we can't touch Him. May we never revel in our heritage that we forget our responsibility. Their spiritual pride and arrogance brought death in the Holy place.

WHAT THE WORLD NEEDS NOW

What the world needs to see is the face of God. This is the grace that is seen by the world in Exodus 33:16 that is endorsed in II Chronicles 7:14. Seeking His face brings a consequence in the church and in the land. There is forgiveness of sin and the healing of the land. When God walks among His people, and His face is seen, there is an outpouring of forgiveness in His house. The

overflow of this glorious power begins to heal the land.

Our land is in desperate need of healing. It is in the throes of disaster and desecration, and the downward spiral is accelerated. I am convinced that worship in His house, and the descent of His power as He walks among us is the key. This is not only the answer to the depression, hurt, dysfunction, and fear around us, but it is the answer to a warring, venomous world that is saturated with animosity.

> II Chronicles 7:16 states, *"For now have I chosen and sanctified this house, that My name may be there for ever: and Mine eyes and Mine heart shall be there perpetually."*

This endorses what I have said before concerning

God's desire to have a perpetual dwelling place where He can walk among His people. God's desire to tabernacle with, walk with and be among His people is so prolific that the purpose for this must be astonishing. You must understand that He is not only in you, with you, but He walks among you.

In Us - Upon Us - Among Us

He is in me, and I know Him as indweller. He is upon me, and I know Him as my anointing. He is with me, and I know Him as my companion. He walks among us, so we know Him as our protector, preserver, as He surrounds us with His presence. It is here that the title of this book, <u>Worship, When God Walks Among Us</u> finds its most potent relevance. I am convinced beyond the shadow of any doubt that the church has an answer to the decay that is around, and I know that God is seeking for a man, or a woman that will transfer the knowledge of His Holy presence to a community, a region, or a world.

Ezekiel 22:30, 31 states, *"And I sought for a man among them, that should make up the hedge, and stand in the gap before Me for the land, that I should not destroy it; but I found none. Therefore have I poured out Mine indignation upon them; I have consumed them with the fire of My wrath; their own way have I recompensed upon their heads, saith the Lord God.""*

The beginning of the healing of the land is contingent on what happens in the house of God. When God stands with me, I can stand against all the vicious attacks of the enemy.

I John 2:15-16 states, *"Love not the world, neither the things that are in the world. If any man love the world, the love of the Father is not in him. For all that is in the world, the lust of the flesh, and the lust of the eyes, and the pride of life, is not of the Father, but is of the world."*

WHAT IS THE WORLD?

The world as we know it is much more than just the sum total of buildings, systems and people. The world is energized by a behind-the-scenes force of the devil and the system that governs the world is fraught with the spirit of the antichrist. There is a presence that is in this world that is heinous and venomous.

It is summarily described in I John 5:18.

"We know that whosoever is born of God sinneth not; but he that is begotten of God keepeth himself, and that wicked one toucheth him not."

The denigration of moral values, the collapse of spiritual ideals, the utter bankruptcy of man-made religion, the erosion of the family, and the propensity to wrong are but symptoms of a deeply spiritual problem.

Deviance and disintegration are only effects of the demonic devilish presence that invisibly animates this worldly system. It is as though they literally walk among the people, the system, and the place. With this in mind, the importance of understanding that God walks among His people is paramount.

I John 5:19 states, *"And we know that we are of God, and the whole world lieth in wickedness."*

Man has willfully and legally sold his soul to the devil by constant indulgence in sin and by his lack of remorse and repentance. When the church is raptured and the Holy Spirit is removed as the restrainer of evil, the entire world will be deluged by demonic power. The saturation of demonic presence will reach its climax.

This possession of the earth is hindered by the presence of the body of Christ and the power of the Holy Spirit. When men choose the path of rebellion, strife, hatred and an abhorrence of godliness, and the acceptance of perverse standards, they authorize the presence of the minions of satan. It is as though man becomes enshrouded in a veil of demonic presence, and these forces surround him and create the atmosphere of anarchy. Men that submit themselves to this macerated form of life do so in a form of worship.

Your Highest Devotion

Whatever commands your highest devotion, that is your god! Giving this unrivaled devotion to sin, becomes worship. This worship of materialism, humanism, and Epicureanism (pleasure seeking) has caused man to be in a place of chaos and confusion. Satan has a jugular instinct, and when he is given this right, he initiates oppression, depression, obsession, regression, and finally possession. This satanic sequence is only authorized by the willful devotion of a seduced soul.

The evidence of an oppressed, obsessed,

possessed society is abundant. Abortion, sexual perversity, teenage pregnancy, the deterioration of the school systems, and moral disintegration are only some of the consequences of a society that is inebriated by satanic influence. This is a time bomb of despair waiting to explode. Yet, in the midst of all of this, there is an amazing alternative. Just as the devotion to and the worship of self and sin, bring this environment of utter bankruptcy, the amazing contrast is that the worship of God brings peace, joy, fulfillment, and purpose. The true worshipper is able to transform his surroundings because now he is not alone, for God walks with him.

SATAN – THE DUPLICATOR

One of the greatest consequences of the ascent of worship is the descent of the Lord and His presence that creates a new spiritual world around us. The atmosphere becomes supercharged with supernatural presence and the enemy's environment explodes with Holy Ghost dynamite. The obnoxious presence of satanic vulgarity does not dominate the space I occupy and his best efforts to distort and destroy are met with immediate abortion. There is an enormously oppressive presence that exudes from a sin filled world system. The presence of spirits of fear, heaviness, infirmities are all around us.

> Ephesians 6:12 states, *"For we wrestle not against flesh and blood, but against principalities, against powers, against the rulers of the darkness of this world, against spiritual wickedness in high places."*

These principalities, powers, rulers of darkness and spiritual weakness are demonic entities that pervade the atmosphere of our world. When the heel of the seed of the woman bruised the head of the serpent (Genesis 3:15), the devil became a duplicator. This means that the enemy stages a drama of duplication to deceive men into darkness, then into destruction. So, the acrostic is simple. Duplication, deception, darkness and destruction.

Let us consider some of the attempts of the devil to duplicate.

1. There is a trinity of God. The Father, The Son, The Holy Spirit. There is a satanic trinity. The beast, the dragon, the false prophet.
2. The Holy Spirit glorifies Jesus. The false prophet glorifies the antichrist.
3. God has a seal. Satan will have a mark.

4. Jesus has a bride. Satan has a whore (Revelation 17).
5. In heaven there are the cherubim, the seraphim, the four living creatures, and the 24 elders. Satan has principalities, powers, rulers of darkness and spiritual wickedness.

LUCIFER – THE WORSHIP DISTORTER

Lucifer understood the power of worship and the effects of worship when he was in Heaven. He has taken this concept, and tried to transfigure it to cause men to be worshippers of himself. When this worship is given to him, whether it is the absorption with self, the chronic dependence on evil, a pornographic mind, or a lusting heart, he is now given the right to dispatch his minions to control and oppress. It is of paramount importance that we understand that the devil is a professional pervert with six thousand years of experience. Men become dithering weaklings, oppressed by demonic presence. I want to declare with unequivocal power that you are created for connection! You are born with a purpose! You have a holy destiny!

You were created to be a worshipper and your destiny is to have God walk with you and among you and yours. The universal disease called loneliness has become epidemic. Its relative, depression, has almost become an institution, and the feeling of isolation inundates the world. The answer to these three evils is found in the heart of true worship. Satan's seductive strategy is to formulate a substitute worship system. Satan's attempt to create a

duplicate worship that gratifies self, exhibits his fear of what true worship is and does. When we worship our focus is fixed, our vision is undiminished, our hearts full and our spirits energized. I am ready to give a depth of worship to my sovereign God that I have never given before. No duplicate or substitute will detour me from the main goal of my life, and that is to be a worshipper! When we get to this place, God walks among us!

THE WORD – THE FLESH
THE DWELLING

John 1:1 states, *"In the beginning was the Word, and the Word was with God, and the Word was God."*

There are some great revelational truths that are incorporated into these scriptures. In the beginning was the Word and this must be understood. When God created the world, Jesus the Saviour was not necessary. He was the Word, and this Word was the very essence and nature of God. This Word was with God and He was God. There was no division in the mind of the godhead concerning the Word. God had a purpose before the foundation of the earth to redeem fallen humanity. He knew when Adam and Eve were created there would be a fall. In the mind of God, before creation, the Lamb was slain before the very foundation of the earth. We must begin to see God's plan in its pre-creation nature. God's purpose was to send the Saviour whose name would be Jesus, for He would save the people from their sin. To accomplish this, the Word had to BECOME flesh.

The Word with all the power and divinity could not be the Saviour of mankind in Heaven. That Word had to become Jesus, and become Jesus in the flesh. The question now arises, how could the Word become flesh? Another question that must be asked is, Why would the Word have to become flesh? Let me answer the how. The word had to become flesh by the conception through the Holy Spirit and the birthing through a woman. The Spirit of God had to be the one who overshadowed Mary, and that which was conceived in her would be Holy. If the Holy Spirit does not move, if the Holy Spirit does not overshadow us, then what is born in us is not birthed from above.

Reception leads to conception and this decides my direction. There are so many people who have followed the wrong direction and this is because of worldly conception and carnal reception. If the world with all its taunting tentacles, torments, traumatizes, and is allowed association and contribution to my life, then what is birthed within is spawned from the belly of hell. With his full armory, the devil mounts an attack of unerring accuracy, pointed deception, and carnal camouflage to reduce my life to ashes of satanic submission. He will reproduce in me the rebelliousness, ruin, venom and viciousness produced by his fall. When my life offers reception to the devils temptations, then the conception of these horrors are the initiator of my direction.

BORN FROM ABOVE

Born from above; there are so many things in church life that are coming forth that have nothing to do with The Father, The Son, or The Holy Spirit. In order for God to bring the Word from Heaven to accomplish the mission of salvation, the Holy Spirit had to be the Daddy. The Word had to be conceived, birthed, and then follow the process of life.

I will come back to this point. Now I will answer the why. The Word became flesh, so He could "Dwell

Among Us". In order to have the abiding presence, the "among us" identification, Jesus had to be birthed in the flesh. For the Word to become flesh that means He was not flesh. When this happened, we could see the glory of the Father.

> John 1:12, *"But as many as received him, to them he gave power to become the sons of God, even to them that believe on his name:"*

The ultimate purpose of the birthing of the Spirit and the travailing of Mary, was Jesus becoming flesh and dwelling among us, so that the glory of the Father could be seen. There is a manifestation of God's glory that is unsurpassed when God dwells and walks among us. Think about the instances in the gospels when Jesus walked and funeral processions were stopped, the blind saw, and the deaf heard. Demons trembled at the presence of Jesus. Spirits cried out in the synagogue. A dead man rose from the tomb. All this came because the Word became flesh to dwell among us. Let me give a spiritual parallel to this. There is an increase of the presence and activity of the Holy Spirit in the Body of Christ.

As hungry, thirsty saints cry out for the move of God, the Spirit of God is moving, brooding, overshadowing just as He did on the day of creation and as He did with Mary. When this happens, Holy and divine things are conceived. When these things are conceived, it leads to travail and birth. I believe with all my heart that Holy things are beginning to be birthed through those who are Word taught, Blood bought and Spirit sought. There are some things that God wants to bring out of the spirit realm into the realm of physical reality, and before this can happen it must become flesh. God's method is men and women. He will send His Spirit and divine conception will take place. Oh, for a heavenly conception! Oh, for a God sent progression. Oh, for the banishment of the devil's deception. God is sovereignly changing the direction of the seeking saint and now the devils plan for weakness, pain, and oppression has been cancelled by a divine conception. It is not within the heart of a man to direct himself, the Bible says, so God now initiates a holy, hallowed, future instead of a hideous, howling tomorrow.

THE BIRTHING AND THE DWELLING

I believe as Jesus became flesh and dwelt among us, so there is a birthing and there will be a dwelling. It is not an enigma when people in whom the Spirit of God dwells and moves, find themselves in the midst of storms, trials, and reversals. I am convinced that before the birth of divine and Holy things, a time of pain precedes it. Jacob had the running, escaping life before the transformation at Peniel. Moses had the running from the palace before the profundity of being the prophet. Elijah had the dying at Cherith before the showing at Carmel. Gideon had the fear of the enemies and no concept of his worth before the angel came. Daniel was called to interpret a dream that led to blessings, in the midst of Belshazzar's attacks. Shadrach, Meschach and Abednego were called to promotion after they were in the fire. Jesus had His Gethsemane and cross before resurrection. Before the exaltation there was an emptying.

The enemy will do all he can to pierce you with problems before God lavishes His mercies on you. Trials before triumph, buffeting before blessings, and violence before victory are not irreconcilable facts. They are actually the sides of the same coin. When you feel like a bull's eye has been tattooed on your body, and the enemy constantly has you in his gun sights, it is time to rejoice.

THE PROCESS - THE POWER

As a student of the prophetic word and the

powerful plan of God for the climax of the ages, I know that there will be a latter day outpouring of the Holy Spirit. God will never allow the lamps of divine witness to be extinguished by the adverse winds of humanism, secularism and materialism. When these lights seem to flicker and are within a hair's breadth of being blown out, God will raise a standard. God's method has always been and will always be men and women. All through the scripture and modern history, men and women have been raised to be vessels, fitted by the Master so a sovereign intervention could be implemented. They were human conduits of a divine plan. They were clean channels for Christ's calling. They were willing worshippers in a chaotic cauldron.

Whenever God is about to send this type of move, someone pays the price of death to the flesh to be alive in the spirit. There is a process before the product. There is preparation before power. There are some who believe the presence of pain, and the advent of adversity betray the weakness of faith. Please consider that God is about to send a dwelling among us. Glory! The pain or adversity could be a part of the birthing process.

Chapter 4

Summary

1. One of the great scriptural truths from Genesis to Revelation is God's desire to walk among us.
2. In Genesis, He walks with Adam and Eve and in Revelation, He tabernacles with His people.
3. The church wants to see the power of God's hand, but He wants to show them the glory of His face.
4. My face must be hid, so His face can be seen.
5. God is in us, upon us, with us, and among us.
6. The beginning of the healing in the land depends on what happens in the church.
7. The world is a place, a system, and a spirit.
8. Satan is not an imitator but a duplicator.
9. Lucifer understood worship, so as satan, he tries to distort it.
10. The Word of the beginning had to become flesh to manifest God's presence.
11. There is a birthing and a dwelling, and the process brings the power.

Chapter 5

The Ark of the Covenant: The Heart of God

The Hebrew word for Ark is *Aron*. This means the chest or the heart. What the ark represented, whatever its purpose, it was a reflection of the heart of God. This is the very thing that the body of Christ must understand. If we could understand what the heart of God is, we would see the hand of God. There are so many who want the power of His hand, without understanding the yearning of His heart. Let us examine the Ark of the Covenant in the context of the heart of God and see how it relates to worship, when God walks among us.

The ark with all its illustrious history and unprecedented symbolism was the most profound of all symbols of the Lord Jesus Christ. If the parallel is to be understood, we must note that what Jesus was to His body in the New Testament, the ark was to the nation of Israel. The ark was the most revered, respected and reverenced object in the tabernacle. So in the body of Christ, Jesus is the head and He is reverenced to the Utmost!

The Ark and Jesus Parallels

The ark symbolized the presence of God "AMONG" the people of Israel. In the New Testament, where two or three are gathered together in My name, I AM "IN THE MIDST", or among them. As long as the ark was in the camp, no enemy was able to destroy them. As long as Jesus is at the center of our lives the enemy is powerless to destroy. The ark represented the rulership, the reign of God in the camp of Israel. Jesus represents the reign of God in the body of Christ. The ark represented the revealed glory in the Holy of Holies that was called the Shekinah glory.

Jesus represents the revealed glory of God to the church.

John 1:14 states, *"And the Word was made flesh, and dwelt among us, (and we beheld His glory, the glory as of the only begotten of the Father,) full of grace and truth."*

The Ark of the Covenant was made of gold and wood, symbolizing the divinity and the humanity of Christ. The gold, the divinity, had to be clothed in flesh, to dwell among us. Think of this holy, hallowed divine precedent. This Jesus was both God and man, yet dwelt among us. The purpose of this intricate plan that was born in Heaven was to create the "dwelling among us" presence.

JESUS THE GOD/MAN

Think about the glorious implications of Jesus being God and man, gold and wood dwelling among us. Let us examine some points on this revelation.

1. As man He is born; as God He is worshipped by the wise at His birth.
2. As man He lies in a manger; as God His birth is announced by angels.
3. As man He sleeps in the storm but as God He rises and rebukes the wind.
4. As man He thirsts but as God He says, "I am the living water."
5. As man He weeps at Lazarus' tomb but as God He commands Lazarus to rise.
6. As man He says destroy this temple but as God, He says, "In three days it will rise."
7. As man He hangs on the cross; as God He opens Heaven for a dying thief.
8. As man He is buried and wrapped; as God He rises in power and glory.

GOD UNDERSTANDS

When Jesus ascended, He ascended as the God-man. He is at the right hand of the Father with full understanding of the trauma, trial, and trepidation that we face. But now, He will walk among us as sovereign God and will touch us at the very focal point of our weakness. **"GOD UNDERSTANDS."** You must remember that this Ark of the Covenant, in its constitution, in its purpose, with all that was within it, graphically exhibited the heart of God. When the ark was taken on its first movement from Mt. Sinai, it was leading the procession in a trip seeking rest for a nation. This journey lasted three days. (Numbers 10:33-36) There is a magnificent parallel with this three day journey and the august accomplishment of our Lord Jesus Christ. He took His people to a place of rest and victory based on His three days and three nights in the grave. The Ark of the Covenant was the symbol of the tangible presence of God among His people, and when this ark was lost, immediate defeat came to Israel.

THE ARK AND THE ARTICLES

Let us consider the paramount importance of the ark and the articles that were in the Ark to the quality of spiritual life that is accessible to the church. Within the Ark of the Covenant were three articles that are reflective of astonishing parallels to the believer today. These articles were two tables of stone containing the Ten Commandments, the golden pot of manna and the budding rod of Aaron. The Ark of the Covenant was called the ark of the testimony, the tables of stone were called the tables of testimony, and the tabernacle was called the tabernacle of testimony. This was a declaration of who God is and what He would reveal if you followed Him. The ark and the articles were a testimony to the guaranteed performance of God. He will do it! Upon the examination of the articles within the ark, there is a fascinating tapestry that is woven that describes the life of Christ and what He would mean to the Christian.

THE LAW – THE MANNA – THE ROD

The law testified of righteousness and Jesus now represents the law of God in my life. Because of this, all of the affairs of my life are governed by this Holy law. Jesus is my law. The pot of manna testified of miraculous sustenance and now Jesus becomes my bread of life. My sustenance is not derived from anything that is external, so the challenges that are around me do not militate against my growth. Jesus is the sustenance, the bread of life to me. The third article in the ark was the rod of Aaron that budded and this budding authenticated His Priesthood. So too, Jesus, the rod that died, budded, on the third day and rose again. This resurrection life authenticated His eternal priesthood, and now the only measuring rod for my life is Jesus. He is my life. There is no circumstance that authoritatively defines my life. There is no riddle, puzzle, challenge or intrusion that can reduce the quality of my life because my

life is infused with and energized by the resurrection life of Jesus. The ark in its representation as the presence of God among the people yesterday accurately describes the power of God walking among His people, today.

OUT OF EGYPT – INTO CANAAN

God brought the nation of Israel out of Egypt by blood, but He would take them into Canaan with the ark. God never brings you out to leave you in a vacuum. Let us examine the enormous implication of entering into Canaan.

1. To get into Canaan, there was a river with an overflowing flood.
2. Jericho, the Canaanite stronghold was before them.
3. There were giants in the land.
4. There were seven nations that were experienced, well-trained warriors.
5. These nations were in union to destroy Israel.
6. Everything that Israel needed was in this land that was well guarded by the enemies.

In order to see victory, to see the defenses of the enemy depart, and to possess their inheritance, they had to become rightly related to the ark. They had to understand that crossing the Jordan, victory at Jericho and throughout Canaan was integrally related to the Ark of the Covenant. Please understand that victory in the life of the believer fully depends on his relationship to Jesus.

There has been a historic fight begun since the garden of Eden and extending to the coming Battle of Armageddon to disrupt and distort relationships. Families, friends, and the relationship to the Father has been violently attacked with vitriolic hatred because the enemy understands the power of balanced, wholesome relationships. He understands that relationships submitted to God become the open door for healing in all other relationships.

The ark represented the dwelling presence of God. Being rightly related to the ark was symbolic of the worship of the people. When this took place, there was victory in the camp because God was their preserver, protector and power. He walked among them.

THE PRIEST - THE ARK
THE FOLLOWER

Joshua 3:3 states, *"And they commanded the people, saying, When ye see the Ark of the Covenant of the Lord your God, and the priests the Levites bearing it, then ye shall remove from your place, and go after it."*

To cross the Jordan, the people had to learn to be followers. When they saw the ark and the priest, then they were to leave that place. The only basis for onward movement was obedience to the word to follow the ark. The priority of Israel's life was the ark. This is a point of paramount importance to the church today, because many have become worshippers of themselves existing in the domain of self absorption. The most dangerous deviation has resulted. But this is the time when God is saying to His people to arise, get up, remove yourself from this place. Regardless of the prohibitive obstacle, or the deep, bridgeless river, or the physically insurmountable walls of Jericho, this is the moment to follow the priest and the ark.

This was their command. When you see the priest and the ark, it's time for the movement of the nation. The enemy will do all he can to hinder you from seeing the priest, to disconnect you from the ark. The ark was borne on the shoulder of the priest being a perfect symbol of the Great High Priest that carries in Himself the presence of heaven.

The river Jordan would be separated when the priest would bear the ark and walk into the river. The bearing of the ark cannot be separated from the presence of the priest. There is no law without the lawgiver, no life without the life- giver, no healing without the healer, no peace without the Prince of Peace. There must be right relation to the priest to have the presence that what the priest offers. When they were going through the Jordan, their eyes would be on the priest.

The Ark, The Center of Life

Joshua 3:11 states, *"Behold, the Ark of the Covenant of the Lord of all the earth passeth over before you into Jordan."*

In crossing the Jordan, everything centered around the ark. In crossing obstacles that are humanly immovable, everything centers around Jesus. As the priest touched the muddy water of the Jordan, the water began to recede. As Jesus died and the words, "It is Finished", were spoken, the deep, murky, forbidden waters of sin receded. The priest, with the ark, stood in this cold river until everyone had passed over. Jesus hung on the cross of Calvary and there He fulfilled the type of the priest, where He stood in the cold river of sin and death and fulfilled His mission so that all could now pass over.

Remember, the Ark of the Covenant reveals the heart of God, and it is an astonishing parallel to Jesus. The threat of death, the frigid water that could cripple a nation did not matter because the priest and the ark were present. God was with them, and God was among them. They had been brought out of Pharaoh's hands by blood. They would enter into their inheritance and destroy the enemies because of the presence of the ark. God would walk among them. When they would enter Canaan their command was not to win the war but to drive out the enemies. Flesh could not boast of this victory, human strategy could not revel in success, as the battle had already been won! The promise of God had already been given, so the presence of God could dwell. For wherever the promise is given, the presence of God leads. When God walks among us, enemies are dispatched without negotiation, and where God points, His power is seen. The presence of well trained marauders did not affect the progress of the people following the ark. The devil's attempt to disconnect you from the ark only shows his fear of the presence of God.

THE FLESH AND FALSE WORSHIP

When the fleshly appetites of life are appeased and the will bows to the influence of carnality, the renegade soul is exercising its right to worship. The satisfaction of the flesh by the consent of the will is a type of worship. This type of worship is in dramatic opposition to true worship, which comes from the spirit. The soul attempts its dominance to produce a deceptive duplicative substitute to spirit worship. The worship through the flesh attempts to bring fulfillment by engaging in the depths of depraved human nature. True worship comes from the spirit. This worship brings the truest and purest fulfillment in the depths of the inner man. Satan's snare of deception though, is subtle, and man has fallen into the trap of self appeasement. This is an abysmal pit of no satisfaction, and society has found itself on the brink of moral, emotional and spiritual extinction because of fleshly indulgence. Because true worship is a fulfillment of my deepest needs, flesh worship attempts to fulfill superficial needs. The flesh touches the soul but the spirit touches the depths of the inner man. The strategy of the enemy is not to drown men by the obvious but to seduce men to engage in duplicity.

DECEPTION, SATAN'S INWARD TOOL

There are two areas of satanic operation that function in this subtle attack to command the worship of men. These areas of operation are deception and seduction. Deception is the devil's operation to control me inwardly while seduction is the devil's operation to control me outwardly. They are carnally connected to the same force, and that is the force of my flesh. There is never deception without seduction. When the devil deceives someone into thinking, or feeling then seduction compels them into acting. Just as holiness and truth are godly operations that take the child of God into blessing, deception and seduction takes men into darkness and destruction. Holiness touches on the inside and truth on the outside and they both bring cleansing and deliverance. So too, deception and seduction bring bondage and imprisonment on the inside and the outside.

This superficial, carnal, engagement of my flesh that has brought so much death and destruction is the devil's bid to detour and distract my true worship. There are so many people in the church who profess but don't possess. They talk it, but they don't walk it. They have formality without content, form but no force. Their lives are filled with the artificial, and they are men pleasers not God pleasers. They try to carefully construct a reputation instead of developing their character. They major on external appearance, but within their lives there is a den of iniquity. The inclination and propensity of flesh worship is to have an emotional, soul filled experience that is vacillating and vacant, with no depth or conviction.

Even though this is an affront to God and an obnoxious substitute, the surface Christian finds this acceptable. The devil deceives, darkens and destroys and the deception of the enemy comes long before the destruction begins. Deception and seduction are the main weapons in the godless trek to false worship. Without the subtlety of inward deception, there can be no outward destruction. If true worship creates the path for God to walk among us, then false worship creates a path for ungodly spirits of fear, heaviness, depression and infirmity to walk among us. This could be the main reason for so many oppressive powers that surround people in the church.

DECEPTION DESCRIBED – THE SOWING AND THE REAPING

Let me examine this two fold cord of deception and seduction.

> Galations 6:7-8 states: *"Be not deceived; God is not mocked: for whatsoever a man soweth, that shall he also reap. For what he soweth to his flesh shall of the flesh reap corruption; but he that soweth to the Spirit shall of the Spirit reap life everlasting."*

When someone thinks he can sow fleshly seeds and have no reaping consequence, he is deceived. I cannot sow wild oats and expect crop failure. When someone sows and does not expect a harvest, this is deception. The scripture states that sowing to the flesh brings corruption from the flesh. This is in keeping with the concept of false worship, and its relation to the flesh, deception and seduction. This flesh life that has been exposed is not the flesh that is exterior. It is the connection with Adam, the carnal nature, the inclination to the "I" life. It is the internal morbidity of a depraved nature that is in constant battle with my new nature.

> Galations 5:17 states: *"For the flesh lusteth against the Spirit, and the Spirit against the flesh: and these are contrary the one to the other: so that ye cannot do the things that ye would."*

When by a conscious act of my will, I sow to my flesh then out of the realm of that flesh I will reap corruption. The worship of flesh only brings corruption. This is where the enemy batters the carnal life. He surrounds it with decay and decadence. The flesh is at enmity with God. It is against God, and it cannot please God. The engagement of the flesh brings the disengagement of blessing.

THE NO SIN LIFE

I John 1:7-9 states: *"But if we walk in the light, as He is in the light, we have fellowship one with another, and the blood of Jesus Christ His Son cleanseth us from all sin. If we say that we have no sin, we deceive ourselves, and the truth is not in us. If we confess our sins, He is faithful and just to forgive us our sins, and to cleanse us from all unrighteousness."*

If we say we have no sin, we deceive ourselves. If we love our sin, there is no need for the cleansing blood and the application of the cross, which is the crucifixion of my flesh. My life becomes a crossless life. The diabolical deception is the elimination of the power of the blood and the crucifixion of the cross. Operation in the flesh will never point to the sin of the flesh. This deception brings the life into a position where there is no need for dependence on God. Life is now bloodless with no cleansing and cross less with no crucifixion. This gives the flesh the avenue to be renegade. The Bible calls this "no sin" scenario, deception. The deception to darken and destroy now becomes evident. Darkness is a consequence of this deception, and this brings destruction. The flesh realm is a bottomless pit of pain and horror, of appetites without satisfaction and craving without fulfillment.

James 1:22 states: *"But be ye doers of the word, and not hearers only, deceiving your own selves."*

To Hear and Not Do

If I hear the word and it is not translated into doing the word, then I have entered a state of deception. When the word comes into my mind and my mind is disoriented or ruled by flesh, then I have no desire to translate the word of God into action. The word does not take root in my life because my flesh ravens eat up the seed of the word. The inability of so many to be hearers and not doers only endorses the fact that they are dominated by an internal flesh life. This deception is internal. It is only the Spirit of God who resides in us that gives us the ability to deal with the force of internal flesh dominance. It is the application of the word to my mind, heart and body that brings transformation. The flesh is the unholy obstruction to this process and will stretch all its tentacles to abort this transformation. The doing of the word establishes the lordship of Jesus and brings a dimension of heaven's power in us and around us.

Luke 6:46-49 states: *"And why call ye Me, Lord, and do not the things which I say? Whosoever cometh to Me, and heareth My sayings, and doeth them, I will show you to whom he is like: He is like a man which built an house, and digged deep, and laid the foundation on a rock: and when the flood arose, the stream beat vehemently upon that house, and could not shake it: for it was founded upon a rock. But he that heareth, and doeth not, is like a man that without a foundation built an house upon the earth; against which the stream did beat vehemently, and immediately it fell; and the ruin of that house was great."*

THE POWER OF DOING

This dynamically illustrates the power of doing the word of God. This application from hearing to doing is likened to a man who built a house and went deep to establish a firm foundation that made his house immovable. No wind, flood, or power could unearth his foundation for it was built on a rock. Our lives are as a spiritual building that has been constructed. Our foundation was dug deep into Calvary where we were founded on the rock, Jesus Christ. He that heareth and doeth not is likened to a man who built a house with no foundation for he built his house on the earth. When the flood came the house immediately fell, and the ruin was great. This person who hears but does not do the word has his home resting on the earth, and his connection to the earthiness, worldliness, and fleshliness caused his weakness. The infection of the earth caused the defection of his life. So when adversity came his house fell immediately, and the ruin was great. This description of a fall and great ruin is an indictment of the flesh. The engagement of life in the flesh is a prescription for disaster. This aspect of deception is one of the most devastating of all for it pretends to be a part of the "word group". It boasts, I have heard the word. Church pews are strewn with internally wrecked lives that boast that they have heard the word. There is a spiritual arterial blockage that restricts the flow of the word from the head to the heart. There is information but no transformation. The informed are the hearers and the transformed are the doers.

DECEPTION
THE DEVIL'S PRIMARY WEAPON

I have devoted this time to deception for it is the flesh's primary weapon, and from the womb of deception flows all evil. When there is true worship, it prepares the way for God in His glory, His attributes, and His power to walk among us. This seems to be a distant, unreachable experience for so many who sit in church because their lives have been disconnected by fleshly deception. Now the purposes of flesh and deception are unveiled. The enemy knows that a life that takes the word from hearing to the doing becomes firmly founded on the rock, and he is now impotent to destroy this life. To the contrary, a life that is fleshly and superficial has no foundation and is now a puppet in the hands of the devil. This puppeteer act of the devil is his desire for the hearts of man. The ultimate aim of this worship of flesh is the acquisition of a controlled, manipulated mankind. This is the ultimate purpose of a flesh-driven life.

SEDUCTION, SATAN'S OUTWARD TOOL

I Timothy 4:1 states: *"Now the Spirit speaketh expressly, that in the latter times some shall depart from the faith, giving heed to seducing spirits, and doctrines of devils."*

This is an insightful revelation concerning the latter days and the operation of seducing spirits. The operation of this seduction brings a departure from the faith for this seduction is the external work of the enemy. Those who were in the faith were dislocated by the force of seducing spirits and became involved with doctrines of devils. In the faith, there is the operation of the Holy Spirit and the presence of the holy doctrine. When there is a departure from the faith, there is the presence of the seducing spirits and unholy doctrines. This seems to be satan's strategy in the latter days as he zeroes in his minions to bring a defection from the faith.

Webster's dictionary gives this definition of the word seduce. "To persuade a person to act contrary to the principles by which he normally abides, to lead astray or away." This outward tool of the enemy is the precursor to deviant behavior. It leads to a life of the relentless pursuit of the flesh. After deception weaves its web on the inside, seduction takes the deceived life into acts of betrayal and sin. This is the extent to which the devil will go to involve the weak and fleshly in a duplicate worship, so that their lives will be filled with horror.

Flesh Manifestation

Galations 5:19-21 states: *"Now the works of the flesh are manifest, which are these;*

Adultery, fornication, uncleanness, lasciviousness, idolatry, witchcraft, hatred, variance, emulations, wrath, strife, seditions, heresies, envyings, murders, drunkenness, revellings, and such like: of the which I tell you before, as I have also told you in time past, that they which do such things shall not inherit the kingdom of God."

This verse gives a list of fleshly operations that become the putrid air that men breathe when their lives are dominated by carnality. All these manifestations literally pervade the atmosphere of life as men bow to the shrine of self and give to the enemy a worship that brings his presence among them. There are so many that speak of the heaviness, strife, and resentment in their lives; this is only a manifestation of flesh absorption as directly described in Galations 5. There is a divine answer to this pervasion of the atmosphere with pain and sorrow. God's will is to find a place to dwell with men and to work in them, through them, and among them. Just as depression, oppression, and obsession can fill our surroundings causing people live under the yoke of the bondage; so too, God can come among us and fill our lives with blessings, hope and glory. True worship prepares the way for God to walk among us.

CHAPTER 5

SUMMARY

1. The Hebrew word for Ark means the heart.
2. The Ark is one of the most profound symbols of Jesus.
3. What the Ark was to the nation of Israel, Jesus is to the church.
4. Jesus is the God/man, all God and all man.
5. The articles within the Ark represent a life parallel to the church.
6. Israel was taken out of Egypt by the blood but into Canaan with the Ark.
7. To cross the Jordan, Israel had to relate to the priest and the Ark.
8. Deception is Satan's inward tool and seduction is his outward tool.

Chapter 6

The Sacrifice and the Sequence

Genesis 15 is a pivotal axis on which Jewish history rotates. Abraham would have experienced serious consternation at the fact that he had no seed to fulfill the promises that he knew were his. The beginning of the chapter presents a perturbed patriarch who is seeking answers to this monumental challenge. It is in this context that a heavenly visitation, a providential interposition, and a divine revelation is about to be given. When pain stabs and unbelief nags, God's word will present truth for today, hope for tomorrow, and the elimination of yesterdays' doubts. What was about to ensue in this chapter could touch the three polarities of Abraham's life: the past, the present, and the future.

God, with a mighty stroke of His omnipotent hand, would work, and the consequence of this divine action would still be seen over four thousand years later. It would mean protection, preservation, purpose, and power to Abraham and his descendants. Abraham came perturbed and puzzled but left covenanted and convinced. He came childless but left with a guaranteed posterity. He came wandering about his future but left edified because of his destiny.

> This is synopsized in Genesis 15:1-5, *"After these things the word of the Lord came unto Abram in a vision, saying, Fear not, Abram: I am thy shield, and thy exceeding great reward. And Abram said, Lord God, what wilt thou give me, seeing I go childless, and the steward of my house is this Eliezer of Damascus? And Abram said, Behold, to me Thou hast given no seed: and, lo, one born in my house is mine heir. And, behold, the word of the Lord came unto him, saying, This shall not be thine heir; but he that shall come forth out of thine own bowels shall be thine heir. And He brought him forth abroad, and said, Look now toward heaven, and tell the stars, if thou be able to number them: and He said unto him, So shall thy seed be."*

A History-Changing Sacrifice

Abraham is about to follow the laws of sacrifice. He is about to worship his God. The response of God to this act would be a historical precedent that would never be annulled or abrogated by the nations. In order to grasp the absolute enormity of this revelation and see its relevance to "Worship, When God Walks Among Us," we must consider the scripture verses very carefully.

>Genesis 15:9-21 states, *"And He said unto him, Take Me a heifer of three years old, and a she goat of three years old, and a ram of three years old, and a turtledove, and a young pigeon. And he took unto Him all these, and divided them in the midst, and laid each piece one against another: but the birds divided he not. And when the fowls came down upon the carcasses, Abram drove them away. And when the sun was going down, a deep sleep fell upon Abram; and, lo, an horror of great darkness fell upon him. And He said unto Abram, Know of a surety that thy seed shall be a stranger in a land that is not theirs, and shall serve them; and they shall afflict them four hundred years; And also that nation, whom they shall serve, will I judge: and afterward shall they come out with great substance. And thou shalt go to thy fathers in peace; thou shalt be buried in a good old age. But in the fourth generation they shall come*

hither again: for the iniquity of the Amorites is not yet full. And it came to pass, that, when the sun went down, and it was dark, behold a smoking furnace, and a burning lamp that passed between those pieces. In the same day the Lord made a covenant with Abram, saying, unto thy seed have I given this land, from the river of Egypt unto the great river, the river Euphrates: The Kenites, and the Kenizzites, and the Kadmonites, and the Hittites, and the Perizzites, and the Rephaims, and the Amorites, and the Canaanites, and the Girgashites, and the Jebusites."

Abraham prepares the heifer, the she goat, the ram, the turtledove and the young pigeon to be sacrificed. After he did this the fowls came on the carcasses, but Abraham drove them away. This is of vital importance to our sacrifice. Nothing that is on the altar is to be touched by the enemy of our soul. They must be driven away, for the sacrifice, this altar, and the remains of the animals belong to God. With vehemence and violence, the attempts of the enemy to touch our sacrifice must be dealt with. This sacrifice is about to bring a divine, history changing, life changing experience, thus no interruption will be tolerated. Verse twelve states that the sun was going down.

There are so many that feel that the sun is going down on their hopes and aspirations, that and they are doomed to the repetition of the discouraging day. This was not the case with Abraham, because the going down of the sun was only the stage for the rising up of the promise of his son, and seed. In times when personal peril endeavors to grasp the soul of the saint, God is only getting ready to provide His power to bring a holy seed through His Son. The sun went down on the hopelessness and the unbelief of verses 1- 3, and verses 5-21 were about to bring life and promise.

REINTERPRETING THE OBVIOUS

We must reinterpret the going down of the sun to understand that during this time, a divine cradle is established to birth miracles. The sun must go down to close the chapter of wavering and wondering and introduce the time of victory and conquest. The same verse declares that a deep sleep fell upon him. This was not a sleep of escape, fatigue, apathy or discouragement. This was a sleep where physical senses had no domination, so that God could do a work in Abraham and through Abraham. Somehow this factory of the soul, that is fleshly that produces emotional trauma and trouble must be silenced. It must not be allowed to abort the revelation and short circuit the divine possibility.

When Adam was put to sleep, Eve was created. Sometimes for God to reproduce His power through us, He must work in us. This sleep would be divinely ominous for the future of Abraham and his seed. Not only must the going down of the sun be reinterpreted, but this sleep must be seen in the light of divine revelation. When my senses are awake and dominate the landscape of my life, fleshly absorption and turmoil are the consequences. God must provide an atmosphere where He alone will work and bring forth His eternal purpose, so a deep sleep fell on Abraham. Deep, so that nothing could pester him in an attack of his senses. Fell upon him, because God becomes the initiator and Abraham becomes the follower.

WHEN GOD GUIDES, WE DON'T STEER

Many times we ask for divine guidance but then assume the steering position, so we endeavor to make God the follower. You will see the paramount importance of these truths as we get to the eternal consequences that they have had, are having, and will continue to have. Then a horror of great darkness fell upon Abraham. To ensure that this work would be undisturbed, this horror of great darkness came. There is no room for misunderstanding here. The description is graphic, and will allow no human agency to prosper. The going down of the sun, the deep sleep, the horror of great darkness cumulatively have eradicated man's power, pomp, and participation.

These are the times that bring the greatest intervention in our life and produce the most life changing, and life-altering possibilities. In this horror of great darkness, Heaven's light would shine on Abraham, his unborn seed, and then a nation. In this womb of darkness, history would be illuminated. Today, when darkness seems great and ponderous, and horror and heaviness are spawned it could be the beginning of God's sovereign plan. Man's extremity becomes God's opportunity. With the silence of flesh upheaval and the presence of God's plan, greatness is born.

GOD WALKS AMONG THE SACRIFICE

Verse 17 brings an amazing presence to this continuing drama. When the sun went down and it was dark, a smoking furnace and a burning lamp "PASSED BETWEEN THOSE PIECES," or God walked among them. After Abraham's obedience to sacrifice, the sun going down, the deep sleep, and the horror of great darkness, God came and walked among the pieces. First, there was worship as he offered the sacrifice. Then he drove away the enemies who would touch the sacrifice. He was put to sleep, and God came among the sacrifice. The purpose was not just for Abraham to go to God in worship, but for God to come to him in a holy descent. The ascent of the worship was only in preparation for the descent of God. Verse 18 declares that God made a covenant with Abraham that same day saying, "unto thy seed have I given this land." Abraham is asleep, and God makes a covenant with him. In this moment Abraham has no response, because he is asleep. This has an astonishing implication. What God is saying to Abraham is that no help, or participation is needed to bring this covenant to pass because God will unilaterally, all by Himself, just because He is God, guarantee this covenant.

THE ABRAHAMIC COVENANT - GOD'S GUARANTEE

This Abrahamic Covenant would be the touch stone of their faith, the foundation for their land, and the hope for tomorrow. No council, cartel, nation, or amalgamation of armies would nullify this covenant.

No president, Prime Minister, or Premier will rise with edicts to obviate the power of this covenant. No army, nuclear power, proliferated weapons, or union of powers will make this covenant void. It is guaranteed, upheld, and expedited by God Himself. When God walked among the pieces of the sacrifice, He was saying to the world that He would be the surety of this covenant. As we draw a parallel reference, we see the power of God in our lives as we offer sacrifices of praise and worship, and God guarantees the future of our lives. This covenant guarantee was for the present and the future, so too the covenanted tomorrow is never a maze of ambiguity when God walks among us like He did in Genesis 15.

FAITH FOR TODAY – BRIGHT HOPE FOR TOMORROW

His purposes are clear and His presence is near. Our present and future are protected and preserved, and the divine endorsement nullifies the voice of the enemy. Blessed assurance fills our lives, and no negotiation is allowed to decide our destiny. In this covenant, the seed is secure, the land is assured, and its borders defined. This covenanted land of Genesis 15:18 includes Lebanon, part of the coasts of Syria, and goes into Turkey. It includes the Persian Gulf, Kuwait, parts of Saudi Arabia, Iran, and Iraq. In the wars of 1948, 1956, 1967, 1973, the nation of Israel took back some of this land which was taken by those who surround her.

In the millennium period, the thousand year reign of Christ, she will possess all her land. There is no doubt that God is with the nation of Israel, and the God of Abraham, Isaac and Jacob does not slumber. When God walked among the pieces of the sacrifice, He became the sole proprietor, the primary protector, and the divine endorser. The historical attempts of the enemy to destroy the nation of Israel with physically overwhelming odds were met with defeat. This is the divine sequence about which the devil is petrified.

As Lucifer, he had a first hand unique perspective on the primacy of worship in Heaven, where the worship atmosphere is profound. The scenes around the throne are illustrative of the heart of God. Let us examine this throne room experience to further understand the structure of heaven's activities and see how this is the pattern for earth's worshippers.

The Heavenly Worship Scene

Revelation 4:7-11 states, *"And the first beast was like a lion, and the second beast like a calf, and the third beast had a face as a man, and the fourth beast was like a flying eagle. And the four beasts had each of them six wings about him; and they were full of eyes within: and they rest not day and night, saying, Holy, holy, holy, Lord God Almighty, which was, and is, and is to come. And when those beasts give glory and honour and thanks to Him that sat on the throne, who liveth for ever and ever, the four and twenty elders fall down before Him that sat on the throne, and worship Him that liveth for ever and ever, and cast their crowns before the throne, saying, Thou art worthy, O Lord, to receive glory and honour and power: for thou hast created all things, and for Thy pleasure they are and were created."*

These four beasts rest not day and night as they are in the presence of the Almighty, and they sing Holy, Holy, Holy to the Lord who was and is and is to come. The eternality of God brings these beasts to worship as they are overwhelmed by the everlasting, eternal presence of God. The 24 elders fall down before the God of heaven worshipping him saying, "Thou art worthy to receive glory and honour and power". The beasts cry holy, and the elders bow in the presence of God. To understand the holiness and eternality of God is to bow before Him in adoration, and adulation. The devil, formerly Lucifer, was very involved in this worship so he understands its position of primacy in God's operations. There is an invasive attack of the enemy on the worship of the people of God. The purpose of this attack is to interrupt the divine sequence that leads to covenant blessing.

So many in church life have to be pumped, primed, pushed, and propelled to worship when this should be the most immediate and spontaneous reaction to the holiness, worthiness and eternality of God. The chorus says, "When I think about the Lord, how He saved me, raised me, filled me with the Holy Ghost, it makes me want to shout Hallelujah!" To think that my life that is restricted by time, space and circumstance is brought into contact with my Father in Heaven who is eternal, is a stunning thought. The relationship that is developed between the worshipper and God is a union that the enemy cannot sever. The reason that Lucifer was kicked out of Heaven was related to worship, for he no longer wanted to be the worshipper, he wanted to be worshipped.

THE END TIME CHURCH DELUSION

There is an unholy, self absorbed, deluded church scene in the end of time explained in Revelation 3:14-20.

It states, *"And unto the angel of the church of the Laodiceans write; These things saith the Amen, the faithful and true witness, the beginning of the creation of God; I know thy works, that thou art neither cold nor hot: I would thou wert cold or hot. So then thou art lukewarm, and neither cold nor hot, I would spew thee out of my mouth. Because thou sayest, I am rich, and increased with goods, and have need of nothing; and knowest not that thou art wretched, and miserable, and poor, and blind, and naked: I counsel thee to buy of Me gold tried in the fire, that thou mayest be rich; and white raiment, that thou mayest be clothed, and that the shame of thy nakedness do not appear; and anoint thine eyes with eyesalve, that thou mayest see. As many as I love, I rebuke and chasten: be zealous therefore, and repent. Behold, I stand at the door, and knock: if any man hear my voice, and open the door, I will come in to him, and will sup with him, and he with Me."*

I will by no stretch of the imagination do an exhaustive explanation of this text but there are several points that are directly related to the interruption of worship. This church symbolizes the spirit of the age as we approach the coming of the Lord. There is a ferocious flesh assault that is launched upon this church, and only the Holy Spirit can derail this carnal juggernaut. It brings revulsion to God, and it is a menace to spiritual liberty. This flesh dictator must be deposed. Verses 15 and 16 define their condition as lukewarm so God spews them out of His mouth. Their condition brings a nauseating feeling, and they are spewed right into the tribulation period.

The reason for this dramatic and graphic action of the Holy, longsuffering God of Heaven is given in verse 17.

"You say I am rich, I am increased with goods, I have need of nothing."

See the unholy descent to self sufficiency and self worship. See the deterioration to bowing at the shrine of self and committing the deepest form of idolatry within the confines of a church. Oh yes, "The Confines of a Church!" This now becomes an impaling, imprisoning experience. What was destined to be filled with liberty is now filled with lust. What was destined to be filled with love is now filled with lewdness. What was destined to be free is now fraught with foolishness. Their boast of riches and the increase of goods was never an affront to God because he wishes that we prosper and be in health as our soul prospers. It is when they said, "I have need of nothing." This brought the holy indictment on the substitute religion that they portrayed. I have need of nothing. The occupation of flesh; I will do what I want, when I want! The obsession with earthly things is the reason for the lack of true worship. Their poor, flesh filled, carnally conquered lives can only bow to the venomous vicious repressive regime of the flesh.

The "I Am" Substitute

The first five words of verse 17 is a volume of information on the worship of the flesh. *"Because thou sayest I am."* Their arrogant ascent to the mount of their flesh, their subtle drumbeat of self absorption, and their biased behaviour of delusion was summarily given in their boast of "I AM". Here sitting in a church where their gospel was tailored to self, their mission was the ministering of things, and their heart was filled with obsession was a group of people that could not be true worshippers. Here in a place where God could have transformed them, they bowed to a god of self appeasement.

> Exodus 3:13-16 states, *"And Moses said unto God, Behold, when I come unto the children of Israel, and shall say unto them, The God of your fathers hath sent me unto you; and they shall say to me, What is His name? what shall I say unto them? And God said unto Moses, I AM THAT I AM: and He said, Thus shalt thou say unto the children of Israel, I AM hath sent me unto you. And God said moreover unto Moses, Thus shalt thou say unto the children of Israel, The Lord God of your fathers, the God of Abraham, the God of Isaac, and the God of Jacob, hath sent me unto you: this is My name for ever, and this is My memorial unto all generations. Go, and gather the elders of Israel together, and say unto them, The Lord God of your fathers, the God of Abraham, of Isaac, and of Jacob, appeared unto me, saying, I have surely visited you, and seen that which is done to you in Egypt:"*

GOD'S HOLY NAME – I AM

God's name given to Moses to speak to Pharaoh was "I AM". This speaks of the eternality of God as seen in verse 15 where it says this is my name forever. Unchangeableness, immutability, and eternality are attributes that can only be given to God. When a man claims to live the I AM life, he is taking a position that only God deserves. This was the very attitude that Lucifer portrayed in Heaven. Now his attempt is to duplicate and reproduce that attitude in the fleshly, the gullible, and the vulnerable. This Luciperic attitude is oppressive and brutal. The full picture of this attempt to obstruct true worship must be unveiled. Fleshly absorption in the church is not some giddy excursion into fantasy, it is a dangerous liaison with the devil himself.

Exodus 6:1-8 gives some astonishing parallels that confirm the covenant power of former paragraphs.

> It states, *"Then the Lord said unto Moses, Now shalt thou see what I will do to Pharaoh: for with a strong hand shall he let them go, and with a strong hand shall he drive them out of his land. And God spake unto Moses, and said unto him, I am the Lord: And I appeared unto*

Abraham, unto Isaac, and unto Jacob, by the name of God Almighty, but by My name JEHOVAH was I not known to them. And I have also established My covenant with them, to give them the land of Canaan, the land of their pilgrimage, wherein they were strangers. And I have also heard the groaning of the children of Israel, whom the Egyptians keep in bondage; and I have remembered My covenant. Wherefore say unto the children of Israel, I am the Lord, and I will bring out from under the burdens of the Egyptians, and I will rid you out of their bondage, and I will redeem you with a stretched out arm, and with great judgments: And I will take you to Me for a people, and I will be to you a God: and ye shall know that I am the Lord your God, which bringeth you out from under the burdens of the Egyptians. And I will bring you in unto the land, concerning the which I did swear to give it to Abraham, to Isaac, and to Jacob; and I will give it you for an heritage: I am the Lord."

Here again the land, the protection and preservation are linked to God's covenant. When God walks among his people, the devil is rendered impotent to control, and his carnivorous appetite has to be relegated to a place of defeat. The ludicrous, absurd obsession with a personal puerile godhood leads to self imposed exile in a land of no fulfillment.

It's Supper Time, But?

Revelation 3:20 shows that God's purpose was to come in and sup with them. However, His position was at the door knocking to get in. The "I am" life had filled the church so their need for Jesus was eliminated. In many religious, tradition filled, flesh saturated churches Jesus is knocking at the door to get in. He is denied access into the home that was raised for His glory, and now it has become a palace of pleasure and a fountain of flesh. God's intention to walk among this Laodecian church was replaced by a people walking in their own degraded self-hood. Whenever I go to preach, and teach, my heart is filled with humility to know that as I worship my Lord and give Him the glory, He sovereignly chooses to walk among us. I believe when this revelation becomes real and personal, and the danger of fleshly absorption is seen and crucified, we will see dimensions of God's power that we have not seen to this point. Let the church be the church. Let the saint be the saint. Let leadership arise in worship. Let this be the day that true worship comes from us, so that

God can walk among us. I make a personal determination; I will not bow to the shrine of self and to the idols of personal preference. I will not live the "I am" life, placing my carnal desires before all else. The door of the church, the door of my heart, and the doors of my family life will be opened for the King of glory to sup with us, and walk among us.

Chapter 6

Summary

1. Genesis 15 is one of the most important chapters in Israel's history.
2. Abraham's sacrifice of his son was history changing.
3. Sacrifice or worship prepares for miracles.
4. For God to do His work in us, our flesh must be inactive, crucified and dead.
5. The offering of this sacrifice prepared the way for God to walk among the sacrifice.
6. The Abrahamic Covenant became God's guarantee.
7. In looking at the 4 beasts and the 24 elders, we see the heavenly worship around the throne.
8. The end time church delusion of the Laodecian church is present today
9. This delusion brings the "I AM" substitute. Not God is but I am.

Chapter 7

The Ark - The Cherubim, God's Meeting Place

In a previous chapter, we considered the parallel between the Ark of the Covenant and Jesus and its implication for Israel and Jesus' presence among His people. The lid of the Ark of the Covenant was made of pure gold. It was here that the blood was sprinkled on the Day of Atonement. The name mercy seat was not figurative, but it was vastly illustrative of the kindness and the goodness of God to His people. The mercies of God to Israel came, and this was the most precious thing that brought hope and restoration to an entire nation. It was a seat for it illustrated the authority of God as blood was shed upon it.

The law that was in the ark that screamed obedience could not shout accusation because of the sprinkled blood on the mercy seat. The mercies of God endure forever. It was the power of this mercy that was able to keep judgment from destroying a sinful, stiff-necked, rebellious people. This was the mercy seat, and it was made of gold. The rest of the ark was made of gold and wood, but the mercy seat had no wood. The wood represents the humanity of Christ; the gold represents mercy of God characterized by the divinity of Christ. The ability to keep the law from penetrating the mercy of God was divine. When God looked at the blood sprinkled mercy seat, His gaze would not be affected by the law because of the blood on the mercy seat.

BETWEEN THE TWO CHERUBIM

There is another astonishing revelation about the ark represented by the two cherubim that were positioned on the mercy seat.

> Exodus 25:22, *"And there I will meet with thee, and I will commune with thee from above the mercy seat, from between the two cherubims which are upon the ark of the testimony, of all things which I will give thee in commandment unto the children of Israel."*
> Numbers 7:89, *"And when Moses was gone into the tabernacle of the congregation to speak with Him, then he heard the voice of One speaking unto him from off the mercy seat that was upon the ark of testimony, from between the two cherubims: and He spake unto him."*
> Isaiah 37:16, *"O Lord of hosts, God of Israel,*

that dwellest between the cherubims, Thou art the God, even Thou alone, of all the kingdoms of the earth: Thou hast made heaven and earth."

The position of the cherubim is of paramount importance. All the illustrative pictures of these cherubim have them with their heads in a downward position with their wings reaching out, and the tip of their wings touching each others. This creates the idea of a covering over the mercy seat as the outstretched wings over-shadowed the ark. The position of the heads of the cherubim speak of their absolute devotion to God. Remember, this ark was like the throne of God in the midst of Israel. The cherubim are in worship, praise, and undisturbed devotion to the King of kings and the Lord of lords. Their vision is focused, their gaze is fixed, and their worship is pure. As they stand on the mercy seat, made of gold, their only option is obeisance to Him who is merciful. When I see the mercies of God my worship is intensified, not because of what He has done for me, but because in Himself, HE IS ALTOGETHER LOVELY, HALLELUJAH!!! With their heads down and their wings outstretched, a magnificent statement is made. God came and spoke from between the wings of the cherubim.

I WILL MEET YOU THERE

Exodus 25:22 gives powerful insight to the desire of God to dwell and to be among his people. The verse says, *"I will meet you there."* When the condition was met and the position was worshipful, God came down to meet him. Let us consider the instructions given concerning the cherubims in Exodus 25:18-20,

> *"And thou shalt make two cherubims of gold, of beaten work shalt thou make them, in the two ends of the mercy seat. And make one cherub on the one end, and the other cherub on the other end: even of the mercy seat shall ye make the cherubims on the two ends thereof. And the cherubims shall stretch forth their wings on high, covering the mercy seat with their wings, and their faces shall look one to another; toward the mercy seat shall the faces of the cherubims be."*

The cherubim themselves were made of gold but the gold was beaten into shape. There is a wonderful parallel here. As I bow before the Lord on the spiritual mercy seat that is sprinkled with the blood of Jesus, I praise Him through the beatings of my life. This is a gold, a purity, that is hammered out from the oppression, attacks, and onslaughts of the enemy. There were two cherubim. They were on either end of the mercy seat, so they covered the entire area of the mercy seat. There is no part of the operation of God's mercy that should not be covered by the praise, adoration, and adulation of God's people. God had set His people apart so that He could meet with men, to walk among them, but now they had to follow the protocol to prepare the place of meeting. These instructions were explicit, and there could be no deviation from the divine instruction. With all the divine specifications, with all the divine recommendations, there was the ultimate purpose of meeting with and walking among His people. This was the holy culmination for God where He would walk with His people. This is the supreme reality - that God would come in the midst of the tabernacle. All this that was happening in the book of Exodus pointed to Jesus and His indwelling in His church. The Israelites believed the ark was the throne of God among them; this also was of immense importance to the future fulfillment of the indwelling of Christ. When my heart was washed in the blood and my spirit was quickened by the Holy Spirit, the throne of God became substantive within me.

THE ARK AND THE HEART

The contents of the ark became the contents of my heart. The two stone tablets containing the Ten Commandments are now written on my heart. The golden pot of manna symbolizes that Jesus becomes my manna, my food, my bread. Aaron's rod that budded in Numbers 17:1-11, is fulfilled in Jesus, the rod of God, budding from the coldness of death into the glories of the resurrection. God viewed the power of the ark and the purpose of the ark with great seriousness, because this represented His tangible presence among His people. The wings of the cherubim according to Exodus 25:20, were stretched forth on high. With the praise that is within me, I am stretched to the point that no part of me is reserved for private, carnal, fleshly indulgence. This stretching is aimed for the highest place, straight into the arms of the Father. Their wings were stretched like my hands are stretched, but their faces were looking toward the mercy seat.

Here is a picture of awesome glory where the wings are stretched high, but the face looks downward. What a powerful parallel to the praising saint. In the place of praise and worship, my hands are stretched heavenward while my face is bowed in humility and adoration. In this position, I am exalting my Lord and bowing before His mercy. The praise position always reminds me of the mercy seat. There are numerous places in the Bible where the mercies of God are associated with the praise of the people of God. The position of the cherubim on the mercy seat was only a reminder of the throne power that would be available to the praiser. Psalms 136 is a psalm that attaches the mercy of God to many great interventions of the faith.

MERCY AND HIS STRETCHED OUT ARM

Psalm 136:12-18, *"With a strong hand, and with a stretched out arm: for His mercy endureth for ever. To Him which divided the Red sea into parts: for His mercy endureth for ever: And made Israel to pass through the midst of it: for His mercy endureth for ever: But overthrew Pharaoh and his host in the Red sea: for His mercy endureth for ever. To Him which led His people through the wilderness: for His mercy endureth for ever. To Him which smote great kings: for His mercy endureth for ever: And slew famous kings: for His mercy endureth for ever:"*

In these verses mercy is connected to deliverance

from Egypt, the parting of the Red sea, the death of Pharoah and his host, the smiting of great kings, and the list goes on. The ark, the mercy seat, and the devoted cherubim all have a supernatural connection to the worshipping prostrated saint, and the glorious that awaits worshipping warriors'.

CHAPTER 7

Summary

1. The lid of the Ark called the Mercy Seat parallels the mercy of God in us today.
2. God spoke from between the wings of the cherubim.
3. The position of the cherubim speaks of devotion and worship.
4. In the Old Testament many miracles are connected to worship, mercy, and the outstretched arms of God.

Chapter 8

Take Him Up To Let Him Down

Mark 2:1-12 states, *"And again he entered into Capernaum after some days; and it was noised that He was in the house. And straightway many were gathered together, insomuch that there was no room to receive them, no, not so much as about the door: and He preached the word unto them. And they come unto Him, bringing one sick of the palsy, which was borne of four. And when they could not come nigh unto Him for the press, they uncovered the roof where He was: and when they had broken it up, they let down the bed wherein the sick of the palsy lay. When Jesus saw their faith, He said unto the sick of palsy, Son, thy sins be forgiven thee. But there were certain of the scribes sitting there, and reasoning in their hearts, why doth this man thus speak blasphemies? Who can forgive sins but God only? And immediately when Jesus perceived in His spirit that they so reasoned with themselves,*

He said unto them, Why reason ye these things in your hearts? Whether it is easier to say to the sick of the palsy, Thy sins be forgiven thee; or to say, Arise, and take up thy bed, and walk? But that ye may know that the Son of man hath power on earth to forgive sins, (He saith to the sick of palsy), I say unto thee, Arise, and take up thy bed, and go thy way into thine house. And immediately he arose, took up the bed, and went forth before them all; insomuch that they were all amazed, and glorified God, saying, We never saw it on this fashion."

JESUS IS IN THE HOUSE

Mark 2:1-12 gives a powerful revelation of the ascent of faith and worship and the descent to where Jesus was. This act of a few men led to a miracle in the presence of Jesus that brought bewilderment to religious leadership. Verse 1 states that the news that Jesus was in the house was noised abroad. This marks the beginning of the miracle. There are so many churches that cannot say that Jesus is in the house, consequently there is no news that spreads about His presence. Rumors of failure abound, tales of foolishness are spread, reports of hypocrisy are rampant, all because His presence is not with them.

No greater compliment, no greater testimony, no greater attestation could be given than the sentence, "Jesus is in this place." If there must be a rumor spread through your community, let it be that Jesus is there. When flesh broods and breeds in church and people's lives become entangled in webs of carnality, what is noised abroad brings defamation and distortion. Our boast must never be in self sufficiency, ability, or accomplishment. It must be that we are blessed and supremely honored to have Jesus in the house.

Verse 2 is a result of this news of hope that was spread abroad, so they gathered together immediately to the place where Jesus was. The crowd gathered so quickly that there was no room to receive them. The doorway was cluttered with people, and the place was packed beyond capacity. The main attraction and the center of attraction was Jesus. This is a prototype for those who want to see lives touched by the Master's hand. Jesus must be the main attraction, and the focal point of the attention. Talent, ability, and gifts must not be showcased in the house, for these must be secondary to the presence of Jesus. Jesus must have no rival, and His presence must have no substitute. We must strive for this august presence. The striving is in direct relation to the banishment of self and flesh from the domain of God.

He alone has the uncontested right to His house. No other can lay a claim to possession by right and performance. Jesus alone has the right because of His death and the performance because of His resurrection. All other claims are channeled by charlatans, and they must be vehemently and violently denied.

TOGETHER FOR ANOTHER

Verse 3 presents the cumulative effort of four men that was necessary to bring one man who was sick of the palsy. To get to where Jesus was with this man sick of the palsy, four men had to engage in a unified effort. This man was paralyzed, so he lacked the ability to get to where Jesus was. To those who are traumatized by trouble, personal pain and inability, and despair and hopelessness emerge, God will provide a means for the desperate to get to Jesus. These four men are to be noted and emulated. They knew that if they got this man to where Jesus was, he could be healed. They also placed their life in the selfless position of sacrifice to see someone else blessed. They possessed the determination to get there, and they were willing to carry him.

Sometimes someone may have to be carried until he/she is able to see Jesus. This is not a prolonged period that creates false, fleshly dependencies. It is only until the carried person is able to see Jesus for himself. In verse 4, they could not come near to Jesus because of the crowd of people who were around him. These men would not be denied the right to get near to Jesus, and they were not prohibited by the crowd. So many times, people have been hindered from getting to where Jesus is because somebody stepped in front of them, and the entrance seems cluttered. These men decided, if we can't go through, we will go up.

UNCOVERED

Verse 4 says they uncovered the roof. This is an extremely poignant statement in relation to their ascent. They went up, and in going up they were able to uncover the roof, so that the man could be let down to where Jesus was. I will equate this going up to the praise and worship of the saint. There are times when people, opinions, reports, and responses crowd the entrance with prohibition and discouragement. In these moments, my determination is I will go up, for nothing will hinder me from getting to where Jesus is. This yearning in my heart to be where Jesus is will not allow me to be deterred. No detour is acceptable for my mind is fixed, and my heart is filled with the desire to see Jesus.

This ascent that I am equating to praise and worship created the possibility of uncovering the roof. The roof is above you, and it shelters you. This roof has to be uncovered. Whatever is above your life and has sheltered you, will be uncovered in worship. Worship uncovers the lives of men and women, and creates the opening to be let down to where Jesus is. Those who relish the idea of fleshly covering will never be desirous to ascend in worship.

There are so many in church life that have a challenge to their worship and praise. This could be what the fleshly covering has bequeathed to them. Whatever covers or shelters me, or hinders me from getting to where Jesus is must be uncovered. A compromising, carnal, cloistered church would have little desire to go up in worship, for it is in this going up that life is uncovered. This uncovering prepares the way for the upward position and a downward blessing. Verse 4 says when they uncovered the roof, they broke it up. One translation says, they dug through it. They had to rip it up and dig through it to create the opening to get the man to Jesus. There are many false traditions, wrong theologies, and false thoughts that have to be ripped apart. There is so much residue that has covered the lives of men, that has to be dug through. Going up in praise and worship gives us the ability to see the roof uncovered, torn apart and dug through.

It's a "Let Down"

Whatever the enemy has done to place a ceiling on your life must be removed, and torn up. There is now a break through to get to Jesus.

> Luke 5:18, 19, *"And, behold, men brought in a bed a man which was taken with a palsy: and they sought means to bring him in, and to lay him before Him. And when they could not find by what way they might bring him in because of the multitude, they went upon the housetop, and let him down through the tiling with his couch into the midst before Jesus."*

Luke 5:18, 19 gives the same perspective. They must get him to where Jesus was. They must not stay out, and this is a determination that we must all make. I will not stay out. Mark 2:4 declares that they let him down, after they tore up the roof. There must be a tearing up before there is a letting down to where Jesus is. It is your worship that tears up fleshly dominance and carnal conception. The ultimate purpose of all these actions was to get the man to where Jesus was, to place him in the midst.

THE FAITH OF FOUR

When the paralytic was let down to where Jesus was, the response of Jesus was amazing. Verse 5 begins, *"When Jesus saw their faith."* The man was lying before Him in his paralyzed condition, but Jesus saw their faith. He saw the faith of the men who ascended, and then he spoke to the condition of the man who descended. In this ascent of worship, which was an exercise of faith, a miracle was wrought. It is in this verse that the ascent is commended, because it was equated to their faith. The clamoring crowds and the blocked entrance meant nothing to the faith-filled-four. Jesus will always see the faith and the worship of His people. It is in this moment that miracles take place. The faith and the ascent of the four with the paralyzed man was enough for divine intervention. This attitude resonated with expectation. When they brought him, he was paralyzed. When they took him up, he was still paralyzed. When they let him down, he was still paralyzed. When he came to where Jesus was, he was healed! There must be an ascent, then the descent, and then the wonderful hands of God as miracles take place.

RELIGIOUS REASONINGS

Mark 2:6-8 presents the reasonings and religious traditions of the unscrupulous scribes. Bigoted by religion and prejudiced by tradition, they would not understand that Jesus could forgive sins. There are always those who question the miracle, reason out the word of God, and endeavor to discount the supernatural. To this, Jesus had an answer in verse 10-12. Arise, and take up thy bed, and go thy way into thine house. He was riveted to his bed as a paralytic thing but now he is able to arise. Now, he is able to take up his bed, and this is filled with meaning.

It means the thing that has carried you, you now carry it. It would be a visible manifestation that would demonstrate the power of God. The ascent of the four, the descent of the paralytic, and the miracle that ensued were all for the glory of God. Verse twelve said, they were all amazed and glorified God saying, "we never saw it in this fashion". This is the response from the spectator that we long to hear. They admit no skepticism, confess no ambiguity, and are not beset by doubts and fears. They are amazed, for standing before them is a miracle.

Whenever men come into the presence of Jesus, it is the beginning of a divine encounter that will bring comfort, healing, deliverance and blessing. The personal responsibility of determination must be accepted. As we follow the path of ascent and descent, miracles begin to happen. If we do what we can, God will do what we can't. I can ascend. I can uncover the roof, tear it up, let him down, and Jesus can heal him. The message of worship as an ascent, that prepares for a descent, and then God walks among us, is the heart beat of the Father.

CHAPTER 8

SUMMARY

1. The greatest statement that can be made of church or house is that Jesus is there.
2. Four men came together to bring one to Jesus.
3. There are times when someone has to be carried.
4. To bring him in, you may have to go up.
5. The going up is only in preparation for the letting down to where Jesus is.
6. Jesus looked at the faith of the four, and healed the man.
7. Along with the miracle came the reasonings of the religious.

Chapter 9

When God Walks in Your Furnace

King Nebuchadnezzar, full of conceit and self-delusion became the perpetuator of false worship. He then set up an image, and this imperial imposter commanded the people of his kingdom to bow in worship. Failure to comply would result in being thrown into a fiery furnace. Three young Hebrew boys refused to compromise their conviction, sell their soul, or bow to a buffoon. This attitude of resistance incensed the oppressor. The king, with all his royalty and regalia, his pomp and his pageantry, was impotent to make these worshipping warriors flinch. With a banner unfurled and thunder in their voices, their resounding response to the king's edict was "We will not bow".

Lives that are bowed in worship to God will never capitulate to the pressure of circumstance, nor will they do obeisance to false gods. Daniel 3:19 says that the king was full of fury. The very thing he wanted from them was the very thing that was reserved for the heart of God. With unabashed loyalty, they resisted the ferocious assault. It is this spirit born worship that infuriates the devil. Now he has found that there are those who will not be caught in the cauldron of self-gratification, self-absorption and self-indulgence. No temptation will thwart the divine design for the true worshipper. No external assault, circumstantial pressure, or seductive suggestion will discourage or detour these young lions. To ensure that death was certain and destruction inevitable, the king ordered the furnace to be heated seven times more than normal.

Now remember that a miracle of national importance is on the way. Three worshipping warriors must do spiritual battle in an overheated, hell-created fire. Let it be known that the over heating of our trial, suffering, and circumstance is not an indictment to indicate annihilation. Many times the overheating of the furnace is only the result of extreme panic exuding from a petrified enemy. It is not a coincidence that the greatest heat preceded the most profound breakout of God's power.

ALL THE KING'S MEN

Daniel 3:20 states, *"And he commanded the most mighty men that were in his army to bind Shadrach, Meshach, and Abednego, and to cast them into the burning fiery furnace."*

The mightiest men were chosen to execute the task of casting the holy worshippers into the flaming furnace. The king is full of fury; he heats the furnace seven times hotter. Now he chooses his mightiest men to cast the Hebrews into the furnace. The king has done all he can to ensure the extinction of the true worshippers. The flawed logic is, if I destroy the worshippers, I will destroy the worship. If I destroy the worship, there will be no obstruction to the saturation of idolatry. If the worship of my gods is mandatory, then my kingdom is perpetuated and protected. This devilish, diabolical logic from this fraudulent king was the force behind the compulsion to kill these three worshippers.

Verse 22 states, *"Therefore because the king's commandment was urgent, and the furnace exceeding hot, the flame of the fire slew those men that took up Shadrach, Meshach, and Abednego."*

This is an astonishing reversal. The king, after dispatching his mighty men to execute his order, saw that the flaming furnace and the burning death destroyed those who were operating under the king's authority. The order was given by the king. The fire and furnace were created by the king's word. The mighty men who cast them in the furnace were following the edict of the king, yet these kings' representatives were the ones who were killed. What the devil planned for evil, God turned it to good and for His glory. The spiritual application is whoever holds you, regardless of how elevated and authoritative a position, will be destroyed in the presence of our august, majestic, sovereign God. The King of kings and the Lord of Lords defends His sons and upholds them with the hand of His power. These minions that were chosen to expedite kingly authority could not be protected from the flames that were created to kill the righteous. The forces of the enemy that have been dispatched with the singular aim of destroying you will be toasted and roasted by the same flame they created.

The Fall and the Flame

Verse 23 states, *"And these three men, Shadrach, Meshach, and Abednego, fell down bound into the midst of the burning fiery furnace."*

Even though they were bound when they entered

the furnace, their choice was to fall down in the midst of the flame - no complaint was lodged, no bickering started, no murmuring seen. They just fell down in worship and surrender, even though they were surrounded by the fire and the flames.

It is this kind of worship that disregards the external, mocks the oppressor, and relegates feeling to a place of significance that absolutely derails the satanic plans of destruction. It confuses and confounds the enemy, and it astonishes those who surround the attackers. We have used our mightiest men, created an overheated furnace, thrown them in, and in the midst of compounded oppression, we can't stop them from worshipping. Astonished, amazed, appalled, and bewildered are but a few of the words that described the trepidation of the king. His carefully concocted, clever and conniving, calculated and cold plans for the destruction of the righteous were aborted by the King of Kings.

> Verse 25 states, *"He answered and said, Lo, I see four men loose, walking in the midst of the fire, and they have no hurt; and the form of the fourth is like the Son of God."*

After the three Hebrew boys fell down in worship in the furnace in verse 23, verse 24 presents a wonderful consequence that endorses and strengthens the title of this book. When the king and his counselors looked from outside the furnace and saw what was happening inside the furnace, their hearts, lives, and soon to be nation would be divinely impacted. These men were no longer bound. They were loosed, and they were walking in the midst of the fire. The heat, the flame, and the furnace did not make them cower in fear, surrender in exasperation, or succumb to the fiendish king. They were walking as if the fire and flame had no claim to their bodies. But there was another amazing development that imperial authority, the counsel of the wise, and the opinions of the nobles had no explanation for. We put three men in this furnace, but look there are four. They are walking in the midst of the fire, and they have no hurt. Let us examine this closely.

WHO IS THIS FOURTH MAN?

Who is this fourth man walking in the furnace? Who is this person over whom fire and flame have no power? Who dares to walk in a situation that is guarded by the king? Who is this intruder that joins the righteous in the midst of judgment and punishment? The king then responded, he is like the Son of God. Could this be the Old Testament manifestation of the Son of God as He walks among His sons? They had fallen down in worship two verses before, and now there is divine intervention and providential interposition. "The earth is the Lord's and the fullness thereof The sovereign God has the right because of ownership to be wherever He chooses. This fiery furnace, which was the most vicious attack that the enemy could launch, was but a microscopic speck in relation to divine majesty. Worship, and God walked among them. Hallelujah!

THE FIRST REVERSAL

When the fourth man appeared, there was a sequence of events that took place that was amazing and - life changing. The first reversal of the king's power was that these men who were bound were now loosed. Let us remember when God comes among us, whatever bonds, oppression, strategy, or semblance of the enemy is there, it will be pulverized and broken by the presence of God. The bondages that were put on these men by enemies on the outside were now loosed by the presence of the fourth man on the inside. When you come into the place where God is, and you draw nigh unto Him, this position will be your security, your deliverance and blessing. They were loosed in the midst of the fire. How it must incense the enemy to see his most calculated attack only provides the opportunity for the elevation of the righteous!

The Second Reversal

The second reversal of the king's authority was that these men were walking. This symbolizes conquest and spiritual achievement. We will not run from the flame, nor will we submit to discouragement. We know our God is with us, and He is among us.

> Joshua 1:3 states, *"Every place that the sole of your foot shall tread upon, that have I given unto you, as I said unto Moses."*

This walking is of great significance to the present attitude and future blessings of the saint. I will not regress. I will not run away. I will not be overwhelmed. I will walk. These deliberate steps, these purposeful movements, these concerted efforts are but fuel to the enemy's frustration.

The Third Reversal

The third reversal to the king's authority was that

they had no hurt. The purpose of the furnace, the plan of the king was to hurt and destroy the righteous remnant. Here they are walking in the midst of the devil's plan with no hurt. When the Son of God walks among us, the most powerful and profound attacks of the enemy will be ineffective to hurt and destroy the ones who know their God. In a world where hurt has saturated the lives of man, there is an answer that is available as we worship, and God walks among us.

The Fourth Reversal

Verse 26 states, *"Then Nebuchadnezzar came near to the mouth of the burning fiery furnace, and spake, and said, Shadrach, Meshach, and Abednego, ye servants of the most high God, come forth, and come hither. Then Shadrach, Meshach, and Abednego, came forth of the midst of the fire."*

The fourth reversal of the enemy was when the king addressed these three Hebrew boys as servants of the most high God. The implication here was that your God is able to do something that I am powerless to do. He is the most high God that is far superior and more powerful than these other puny, puerile gods. It is this demonstration of the fourth man in the furnace that abrogated the claims of the king, annulled the plans of destruction, and initiated the exaltation of the righteous. The scandalous strategy of the king was summarily cancelled because of the intervention of the most high God. The king had no option but to reverse his opinion of the God of these men.

The Fifth Reversal

Verse 26 states, *"Then Nebuchadnezzar came near to the mouth of the burning fiery furnace, and spake, and said, Shadrach, Meshach, and Abednego, ye servants of the most high God, come forth, and come hither. Then Shadrach, Meshach, and Abednego, came forth of the midst of the fire."*

They were called out of the furnace by the word of the king, and this represents the fifth reversal. It was the king's word of death and destruction that had cast them into this burning death. Now, after the experience with the fourth man, it is the king's word that brings them out. This is an experience that many of God's people will experience as they see God walking among them. The furnaces that have swallowed them and the enemies that have been quick to escort them and dispatch them into oppression will now tell them to come forth. Yes, the word today is COME FORTH! God's ultimate objective is for the carnal, worldly onlookers to see the presence, person, and power of Heaven in us and through us, so that they will know that He is God. Preserved and protected, saved and secure, worshipping not worrying, we are ready to come forth.

The Sixth Reversal

Verse 27 states, *"And the princes, governors, and captains, and the kings counselors, being gathered together, saw these men, upon whose bodies the fire had no power, nor was an hair on their head singed, neither were their coats changed, nor the smell of fire had passed on them."*

This verse represents the sixth reversal and now it includes the governors, captains, and counselors together. They now declare that the fire had no power over their bodies. Not a hair on their body was singed, nor the bodies filled with the smell of smoke. The power of the flame created by a king had no power over the bodies of the worshippers touched by

God. Babylon's power, the king's edict, and the court's ruling was not enough to deal with the power of the protecting, preserving God of Heaven. No residue of the furnace was left on these worshippers, for even the smell of the fire had not touched them. This must be of monumental importance to the righteous who find the furnace experience to be discouraging and disillusioning. Neither the fire nor the smoke has any power over my body. I am in the furnace, not because I have failed and fallen, but because God wants His glory to be seen by the authorities. He wants them to know that all their plans and powers pale into oblivion in the midst of Heaven's glory. He wants them to see from the furnace they created, that the true God reigns.

THE SEVENTH REVERSAL

Verse 28 states, *"Then Nebuchadnezzar spake, and said, Blessed be the God of Shadrach, Meshach, and Abednego, who hath sent His angel, and delivered His servants that trusted in Him, and have changed the king's word, and yielded their bodies, that they might not serve nor worship any god, except their own God."*

This represents the seventh reversal, and seven is the number of spiritual perfection. The verse says, Blessed be the God of Shadrach, Meshach, and Abednego. Now the gods of Babylon are relegated to a position of unimportance, and the God of these furnace survivors are elevated in the midst of Babylon. This verse goes on to describe why the king calls God blessed. 1) He sent His angel 2) He delivered His servants 3) He has changed the king's word 4) His followers would worship no other god, except their God. The king is now understanding and declaring the glories of the God of these men because they worshipped, fell down, and God walked among them. These are the transformations that happen to the critical and oppressive when they see the power of our God walking in our furnace.

THE EIGHTH REVERSAL
A NEW BEGINNING

Verse 29 states, *"Therefore I make a decree, That every people, nation, and language, which speak anything amiss against the God of Shadrach, Meshach, and Abednego, shall be cut in pieces, and their houses shall be made a dunghill: because there is no other God that can deliver after this sort."*

This is an astonishing reversal, and it represents the eighth reversal. The number eight is the number of new beginnings. Now the king makes another decree, which means he has changed the former decree that ordered opposition to the God of Shadrach, Meshach, and Abednego. He changed his word.

This is what the demonstration of the power of God will do for those who stand for the will and plan of God. The king's decree is this. Anyone who speaks, "against the God of Shadrach, Meshach, and Abednego shall be cut in pieces, because there is no other god that can deliver after this sort". What an absolute transfiguration in the mind of the king, which inevitably filters down to the nation and its people. This is where the message of worship, and God walks among us is seen in its truest and most powerful manifestation. Dignitaries, leaders, authoritarians, and the people whom they serve are now exposed to the majesty and might of the true God, because three Hebrew boys worshipped in a furnace and God walked among them.

THE NINTH REVERSAL

Verse 30 states, *"Then the king promoted Shadrach, Meshach, and Abednego, in the province of Babylon."*

This is the ninth reversal of the enemy's plan and the king's word. The same word that was determined to destroy them is now the same word that is promoting them. God will promote the righteous as He sees them in the position of worship in the furnace and faithfulness in the fight. When the righteous are in authority the people rejoiced, so this promotion of the righteous is a part of the plan of God in our day.

This is a divine sequence of events that was initiated that must be defined.

> Isaiah 46:10 declares, *"Declaring the end from the beginning, and from ancient times the things that are not yet done, saying, My counsel shall stand, and I will do all my pleasure:"*

Since God is omniscient and He holds the past, present, and future in the palms of His hand, He sovereignly orders the enemies in the present to serve His purpose for the future. To those who submit their lives to His will, the end has been guaranteed, assured, and sealed. When God begins to deal with those who obediently follow Him, He is working towards a divinely foreordained plan.

It is a wonderful thing that finite beings who have surrendered to the sovereignty of God can be a part of an infinite eternal plan. My flesh with its biased behavior that makes it notoriously difficult to experience God's divine design, is now dismantled and derailed. I feel like liquid fire now flows through my veins as I begin to proceed towards a divine encounter with God's appointed destiny for my life. Later on in Daniel 4, the king because of his arrogant, excessive, and profane behavior would be driven to live with certainly declares the end from the beginning. It is this declaration that guarantees my protection, preservation and exaltation.

A Revelation of Names

I find in the names of these Hebrew holy boys an amazing revelation concerning their future, and an explanation of why the enemy chose to violently assault them. Shadrach means a tender field, Meshach means one who draws with force, and Abednego means a servant of light. When these are put together it carries a profound meaning with powerful permutations. In a tender field, there is one who draws with force because he is a servant of light. This is a picture of a harvest field, with someone empowered with the force of the Holy Spirit and is made a servant of light. In the midst of the fiery furnace and the flaming fire, amidst the oppression and brutality of the leaders, a holy fascinating tapestry unfurls.

These men symbolized a harvest filled with men touched by the Holy Spirit that will draw others and are servants of light. In a land filled with the exercises of fake religion and a licentious mode of worship, God has ordained a tender field. In a land filled with the force of religious deception, God has ordained people, anointed and appointed, that will draw with force. In a land benighted with despair and darkness God has raised up servants of light. The names of the three Hebrews that were assailed and assaulted by the enemy indicated that God's plan was far more powerful than the plan of the king and his followers.

PRE-RAPTURE REFRESHING

In these closing days of time when history seems to be in the fast forward mode and world changing events seem to be happening in 24 hour time periods, I am thrilled to know that God is still manifesting His power. It is my belief, and it has been for years, that before the rapture of the church there will be a supernatural, Heaven sent time of restoration. I believe that the righteous remnant who have not bowed to false gods of ease and materialism, who have not succumbed to the deception of humanism, will rise in God's power. The weak, spiritless, anemic atmosphere in many, will be replaced by a glorious manifestation of God's holy presence and power. Where sin doth abound, grace will much more abound. It is this much power, presence and manifestation that must prevail.

So let the enemies of God concoct their fiendish plots, let them overheat their furnaces of burning death, let the devil devise strategies to cause the righteous to surrender and succumb, they will all abruptly fail. In the midst of the hottest, most fiery trials that will come, the fourth man, the Son of God, will step into the furnace and God will walk amongst us, bringing protection, restoration and exaltation. Protection in the fire, restoration from a furnace, and exaltation in the midst of burning death, and all this because the worship in the furnace invited God to walk amongst them. Be edified, blessed, worshipful, and exalted, for God walks among us.

Chapter 9

Summary

1. There are always those who try to create false worship.
2. The result of non-compliance to the king's command was a furnace.
3. In the furnace there were nine reversals of the king's word.
4. After the nine reversals, a foreordained plan began to unfold.
5. These men were exalted from a furnace.
6. These three names of these Hebrew boys present an astonishing parallel to today's harvest.
7. Be ready for a pre-rapture refreshing.

Made in the USA
Columbia, SC
16 October 2018